NORTH CENTRAL COLLEGE LIBRARY

Naperville, Illinois

Presented by

MRS. ALICE I. ANDERSON
&
ANDREW & GERALDINE M. ANDERSON

In Memory of

MR. & MRS. PEDER ERLINDER

Swetnam the Woman-hater:
The Controversy and the Play

SWETNAM,
THE
VVoman-hater,
ARRAIGNED BY
WOMEN.

A new Comedie,

Acted at the *Red Bull*, by the late
Queenes Seruants.

LONDON
Printed for *Richard Meighen*, and are to be sold at his Shops
at Saint *Clements* Church, ouer-againſt *Essex* Houſe, and
at *Westminster* Hall. 1620.

University of Illinois Library

Title page of the 1620 edition

Swetnam the Woman-hater:
The Controversy and the Play

A Critical Edition With
Introduction and Notes

by Coryl Crandall

1969
Purdue University Studies

Standard Book Number 911198-22-9

Library of Congress Catalog Card Number 69-11982

Printed in United States of America

© 1969 by Purdue Research Foundation

To:

Ruth McGugan

Dana McKinnon

and

Catharine Regan

The world is not all made of otemell.

—Joseph Swetnam

Preface

The purpose of this book is to provide an accessible modern edition of *Swetnam the Woman-hater* (1620), a good Jacobean tragi-comedy; to discuss the controversy which seems to have stimulated the play's writing; and to discuss what I believe that controversy tells us about the attitudes of the time toward feminism and anti-feminism. I hope, as authors and editors of all such presentations hope, that consideration of these specific matters will add also to our understanding of the general spirit of that time, the early seventeenth century.

While preparing this book I received invaluable encouragement and understanding guidance from Professor Allan Holaday of the University of Illinois, Urbana, who read the entire manuscript at various stages. It is impossible to acknowledge adequately the extent of his help. Most of chapter one appeared as "Cultural Implications of the Swetnam Anti-feminist Controversy in the Seventeenth Century," in the *Journal of Popular Culture* (Summer, 1968), vol. 2, no. 1. I am thankful to its editor, Professor Ray B. Browne, Bowling Green State University, Bowling Green, Ohio, for his friendship and encouragement.

As is true in most such cases, it is impossible to acknowledge everyone who has been helpful in some way with this project. I would like, however, to express special thanks to Professor Felix Stefanile, Chairman of the Editorial Board, Purdue University Studies, whose encouragement and interest made this publication possible; to Professor Dennis G. Donovan, the University of North Carolina, Chapel Hill, who read the manuscript and made many helpful suggestions; to Professor Henry Salerno, State University of New York, Fredonia, for his suggestions; to my wife Eleanor, for her personal and professional help; to University of Illinois Librarians Miss Eva Faye Benton, Miss Alma DeJordy, and the entire staff of the Illinois Rare Book Room, for their charm and assistance; to Professors Arthur Barker, Lloyd Berry, and Charles Shattuck, for their friendly comments; and to Miss Karen L. Slattery, Menominee, Michigan, for her helpful assistance.

Needless to say, all the faults here are mine alone.

Coryl Crandall
Green Bay, Wisconsin
August, 1968

Contents

ix	Preface
1	Chapter 1: Joseph Swetnam and his Detractors
22	Chapter 2: Source, Stage History, and Authorship
33	Chapter 3: The Play as Literature and Theater
47	Swetnam the Woman-hater, Arraigned by Women
48	A Note on the Text
53	Actorvm Nomina
54	Prologve
55	Act I
71	Act II
84	Act III
103	Act IIII
118	Act V
140	Epilogve
141	Table of Grosart's Emendations
148	Textual Notes
154	Glossarial and Explanatory Notes
159	Bibliography
161	Index

Chapter 1.

Joseph Swetnam and His Detractors

I.

In 1615, when Joseph Swetnam published the *Araignment of Lewde, idle, froward, and vnconstant women*[1], he could not have realized that his pamphlet would bring him Jacobean stage notoriety. If he had ever envisioned himself on stage, it is unlikely that he had seen himself as the major character in *Swetnam the Woman-hater* (1620).[2] No one would wish to be treated so.

No matter his personal aims, Swetnam and his *Araignment* initiated an anti-feminist controversy that interests us first of all because the nature of the works involved tells us a good deal about the attitudes of the popular reading audience of the time, and secondly because we owe to the controversy the existence of its culminating work, a good and entertaining Jacobean tragi-comedy.

Not much is known about Joseph Swetnam except that he was also the author of a book on fencing, *The Schoole of The Noble and Worthy Science of Defence* (1617).[3] Alexander B. Grosart, in the introduction to his 1880 edition of *Swetnam the Woman-hater*,[4] and Barbara Matulka, in a discussion of the play's source,[5] assume that there must be some truth to the comments made about him in the play, the only source that they depend upon, since all other "sources" clearly derive from one or both of his pamphlets. One assumes, therefore, that if the play is reasonably accurate, Swetnam ran a fencing school in Bristol. In Act I, Scene ii, Misogenos (Swetnam's alias in the play) tells his clown companion, Swash, that they will set up a fencing school in Sicily, "The same we did in Bristow" (57). Later, in Act V, Scene ii, Bristow is mentioned again, this time in a speech by Swash who gives the following, mostly fictional, account.

> He is no Fencer, that's but for a shew,
> For feare of being beaten: the best Clarke,
> For cowardise that can be in the World,
> To terrifie the Female Champions,

1

> He was in England, a poore Scholer first,
> And came to Medley, to eate Cakes and Creame,
> At my old Mothers house; she trusted him,
> At least some sixteene shillings o' the score,
> And he perswaded her, he would make me
> A Scholer of the Vniversitie,
> Which she, kind Foole, beleeu'd: He neu'r taught me
> Any Lesson, but to raile against women,
> That was my morning and my euening Lecture.
> And in one yeere he runne away from thence,
> And then he tooke the habit of a Fencer:
> And set vp Schoole at Bristow: there he liu'd
> A yeere or two, till he had writ this Booke:
> And then the women beat him out the Towne,
> And then we came to London: there forsooth,
> He put his Booke i' the Presse, and publisht it,
> And made a thousand men and wiues fall out.
> Till two or three good wenches, in meere spight,
> Laid their heads together, and rail'd him out of th' Land,
> Then we came hither: this is all forsooth. (300-323)

Whatever kind of a man he was, he probably could not have been as fraudulent as the play makes him seem; the *Schoole* appears to be a sincere and apparently informed work. He says of himself in the *Schoole* that he is "no Scholler, nor haue no learning." He "was neuer at *Oxford* but while I baited my horse; nor at *Cambridge* but while one *Sturbridge* faire lasted" (A4); he does, however, claim credit for experience. His "Epistle vnto the common Reader" and address to the "Possessors of the Noble and worthie Art of Defence" both are filled with homey advice which reflects the general attitude of his anti-feminist pamphlet—that such advice from experienced elders is good: "I would not haue yong sprigs spoiled in the blosome, I meane I would not haue yong branches or young [sic] entereres into the world imbarke themselues away in a manner, before they haue had any beginning" (A4^V). What, perhaps, is most significant to note is that the first 74 pages of this 198-page work are devoted not to the technicalities of fencing but to warnings about drunkenness, cowardice, laziness, complacency, etc. Swetnam was seemingly deeply concerned with practical advice. His work is abundant in proverbs and lessons, and his anti-feminist pamphlet maintains that one of its motives is to warn young men against the dangers of women.

II.

Anti-feminist feeling usually is thought to be strong and wide-spread during the mid and late English renaissance in spite of Louis Wright's observation that

[b]ecause Puritan zealots of the mid-seventeenth century abused women, it is fallacious to assume that the attitude of the rank and file of the middle class was one of opposition to woman's social progress; the same Puritans objected to the theater, music, and all forms of amusements; yet certainly they did not represent the composite opinion of the class of which, at the moment, they were the most voluble part.[6]

The controversy surrounding Swetnam's *Araignment* hints that—in spite of the pamphlet's popularity[7]—the feeling among the majority of the seventeenth century middle class was more reasonable than is usually thought, even earlier than the mid-seventeenth century. Although much feminist and anti-feminist activity followed this controversy, its outcome implies that the prevailing attitude was the one reflected in *Swetnam the Woman-hater;* that men and women are equally guilty of and share the propensity for sin.

Generally speaking, the history and nature of feminist controversy until 1615 would be as difficult to describe precisely as the history and nature of such interest after that date. However, we can safely distinguish between two general interests or concerns manifested in this kind of literature. The first, more common to the earlier works, considers the nature of woman as a being: is she basically good or bad? specifically is she better or worse than man? The second considers not so much what women are, as what women can be (good or bad), and seems more realistically based on the assumption that the sexes are, for the most part, equal in their inclinations to evil. It is often difficult to place literature of the latter concern in a familiar "debate" tradition, whether we conceive this tradition to imply a debate (either in prose or verse) by one person or a controversy among several. Such literature is usually not concerned with a specific anti-feminist controversy which is initiated by one or two strongly provocative leaders and which spawns a series of documents that can be counted and ordered. It is, instead, involved in what we recognize as the ever-present controversy over women. The basic assumption underlying this quieter concern is apparently that women and men, though different, are equally responsible. Professor Wright notes that "out of the controversial [renaissance] literature about women came fervent demands from both middle-class and aristocratic writers for the recognition of woman's equality with man."[8] The Swetnam controversy reflects very well a transition from a previous literary obsession with praise or dispraise of woman *qua* woman to a concern with woman's mundane stature as partner of man.

There were six works involved in the controversy, beginning with the *Araignment* in 1615 and ending with publication of *Swetnam the Woman-hater* in 1620. The other four, probably in this order, were as follows: Daniel Tuvil's *Asylum Veneris* (1616),[9] Rachel Speght's *A Mouzell for Melastomus* (1617),[10] Ester Sowernam's (pseudonym) *Ester hath hang'd Haman* (1617),[11] and Constantia Munda's (pseudonym) *The Worming of a mad Dogge* (1617).[12]

The *Araignment* is by no means an impressive work. The Rev. Mr. Grosart, not unreasonably, refers to it as "without a spark of wit or salt of pungency."[13] Dedicating the *Araignment* "Neither to the best nor yet to the worst, but to the common sort of Women," Swetnam opens with an admission to "being in a great chollor against some women" (1). He claims in this introductory epistle that he does not wish to condemn good women, but hopes "to better the good by the naughty examples of the badd." However, he turns in his very next sentence to say, "[T]here is no woman so good but hath one idle part or other in her" (2). He signs this epistle "Thomas Tel-troth." In a second introductory note, he addresses his work to "the ordinary sort of giddy headed young men." He urges them to read every part of his pamphlet if they "mean to see the Bear-bayting of women" (4).

The body of the work is a disorganized condemnation of women. Although the purpose of chapter one, he says, is to show how women have degenerated "from the use they were framed vnto" to their present "lasie and idle" (7) lives, the chapter consists of little more than Biblical and historical references and "reasons" for the general wickedness of women. It concludes with a warning against marriage and being "snared in womens nets" (17). Chapter two, he says, will show how great men have been ruined by women. However, it includes some stories of notorious women whose whoredom, although bringing them profit, seemed to hurt no man in particular. He spends most of his time discussing the bad luck that Solomon and Socrates had with women. Then he warns against marriage because women are wanton, selfish, and vain. Even when they are beautiful, "shewing pitty, yet their heartes are blacke, swelling with mischiefe, not much vnlike old trees, whose outward leaves are faire and greene and yet the body rotten." He maintains that God made women "to be a plague to men" and that that was the reason He "called them necessary euills" (33).

Chapter three offers "a remedy against loue" and advice—if one feels he must marry—on "howe to choose a wife" (35). The gist of this section is that it is foolish to marry, that "[t]here are six kindes of women" not to marry, "that is to say, good nor bad, faire nor foule, rich nor poore" (37). He repeats a statement he makes earlier, that men have one fault, "drunkenesse," and that women have two, "they can neither say well nor doe well" (38). If one must marry, he should marry "a young woman of tender yeares [who] is flexable and bending, obedient and subiect to doe anything, according to the will and pleasure of her husband." The chapter continues, after stating that "many a man happeneth sooner on a shrew then a ship" (46) to concede that there are some good women, and then he devotes a few pages to the duties of husbands as well as wives. He concludes the discussion with a section on *"The Bearbaiting or the vanity of Widowes,"* in which he warns against marriage "vnto a widowe, for a widowe will be the cause of a thousand woes" (57). Swetnam's pamphlet had to have made him enemies—especially among the women.

Tuvil's *Asylum Veneris,* published the next year, is on one hand the least important in the controversy because there is no evidence, only supposition, that it was published in answer to Swetnam's treatise,[14] and on the other hand the most interesting because of the reasonableness of his approach, generally the same kind reflected in *Swetnam the Woman-hater*. It is also the best written of the pamphlets. Tuvil makes it clear that his work is not addressed to the common people, but to "the learned and the good" (A5^V). He does say in his introduction that there is need for a defense of women: "I know this age to be very Stoicall and Criticall, and that many will censure the Author to haue seriously busied himself in an idle subiect; as making no account of vertue in women, though they come farre short of it themselues" (A5).

Although his pamphlet is a defense, he opens with a poem "To the looser sort of Women."

Stand of you foule adulterate brats of Hell,
Whose lunges exhale a worse than sulph'rous smell,
Do not attempt with your prophaner hands
To touch the Shrine, in which chast Virtue stands. (A8)

The pamphlet cannot be labeled strictly feminist, in spite of Tuvil's ten chapters on "Womens worth in generall," "their Beauty," "their Chastity," "outward modestie," "Humility, and supposed Pride," "Constancie of . . . Affections." Much of chapter one is devoted to the traditional arguments that women cannot be evil beings: "Our Sauiour did not scorne when hee came downe from heauen to make the wombe of a Virgin, the receptacle of his glory" (7). He notes, however, that some women deserve reproach. In chapter two, Tuvil praises the beauty of women, but he warns that "She that hath a faire body, but a foule minde, is like vnto him that hath a good Ship, but an ill Pilot" (21-22). In his third chapter, on chastity, he says that there certainly are unchaste women, but adds, "It were ridiculous for any man to condemne the Rose because there is a prickle in the bush" (32).

And here, it is important to note, he begins to advise women: "Chastitie must haue setled Grauitie for hir Vsher; and for hir waiting-woman, bashfull Modestie; or she shall neuer procure respectiue reuerence and obseruance from those that doe behold hir" (37). Women must not only be modest but look modest: "A booke is censured many times, by what the title promiseth" (38). More and more throughout the rest of the pamphlet, his purpose seems to be to advise as well as defend. Woman should be "chast and frugall, busied still about hir huswiuerie"; "She should not hunt ambitiously after popular applause" (52); she should not "make herself up excessively" (58). He reminds men, not that women always keep secrets, but that as many men as women do *not* keep them (70); he notes that women are as wise as men, not wiser (100-114).

We must recognize, then, that Tuvil's pamphlet is on one hand a defense of women, and therefore in the debate or controversy tradition, and on the other hand an instruction for women, and therefore somewhat in the courtesy book tradition. Instead of arguing, as do most of the sixteenth century defenses, that women are superior, or more virtuous than men, Tuvil's contends that they are equal. Each chapter contains the expected introduction of the charges usually made against women, but the following defense consists of refutation and general discussion of women rather than praise of them.

Rachel Speght's *A Mouzell for Melastomus* is the first of the direct answers to Swetnam's *Araignment*. In the "Epistle Dedicatorie" she addresses herself "To all vertuous Ladies Honourable or Worshipfull, and to all others of Heuahs sex fearing God, and Louing their iust reputation." She must answer because as the viper "vomit[s] forth her poyson, and in the spring time sucketh the same vp againe, which becommeth twise as deadly as the former" (A3-A3^V), so might Swetnam write another pamphlet twice as bad. Also, if it goes unanswered "the vulgar ignorant might haue beleeued his Diabollicall infamies to be infallible truths, not to be infringed; whereas now they may plainely perceiue them to bee but the scumme of Heathenish braines" (A3^V).

In spite of this relatively vehement beginning, Rachel Speght is not as extreme in her defense as Swetnam is in his attack. She is answering Swetnam, she says, because no one else has; however, she is not trying to be presumptuous "thinking myselfe more fit then others" but she is confident and "out of all feare" because she is "armed with the truth" (A4). An acrostic poem follows, the first letters of each line spelling "Swetnam." He is referred to as a "Seducer of the vulgar sort of men" (B1). Although on "your Title Leafe . . . you arraigne none but lewd, idle, froward and vnconstant women," the pamphlet really criticizes them all *"Good* and *Badde, Faire* and *Foule, Rich* and *Poore"* (B3). She says that women, weaker than men, are not more guilty, but perhaps less, of sin, because the guilt of men, strong and enjoying free will, is intensified by their strength. The argument goes on in the traditional manner, using Biblical references to support statements. What makes the presentation less effective than it might be, perhaps, is the major concession that women are "weaker" than men, and less "perfect." She says that "if two Oxen be put in one yoke, the one being bigger than the other, the greater beares most weight; so the Husband being the stronger vessell is to beare a greater burthen then his wife" ($D2^V$). Some of her mildness results because she wishes to be neither feminist nor anti-feminist: "of men as of women, there are two sorts, namely good and bad" ($E1^V$). The epilogue of the pamphlet states that men who are ungrateful to God for the gift of women should be ashamed for their unthankfulness. Swetnam's next opponent, under the pseudonym of Ester Sowernam, was not so polite.

Immediately following *A Mouzell for Melastomus,* Rachael Speght offers *Certain Quaeres to the bayter of Women,* really a pamphlet attached to the first. It opens with an epistle *"To the Reader"* which is signed by the author. She does not want to touch on each of Swetnam's points: "His absrudities therein contayned, are so many, that to answere them seuerally, were as friuolous a worke, as to make a Trappe for a Flea" ($F1^V$). She follows with a "Preface vnto the Subseqnent [sic]" in which she says she wants to make it clear that she does not "finde fault where none is" ($F2^V$). She wishes to set forth some queries. In the text she again cites Biblical and historical evidence in refutation of Swetnam, but this time she calls him on specific points, especially his grammar, with which she is perhaps excessively concerned.

Ester Sowernam's *Ester hath hang'd Haman* is a much better defense of women and a much stronger answer to Swetnam. Unlike *A Mouzell for Melastomus,* the Sowernam pamphlet is not humble; it is feminist. Her purpose is "to proue, that men should honour them [women] for their best dispositions," and that "if there be any offense in woman, men were the beginners" ($A3^V$). And further, *"If you beliewe our aduersary, no woman is good, howsoeuer she be vsed: if you considere what I haue written, no woman is bad except she be abused"* (A^V). Even the admissions that women can be bad are made to prove women's superiority, and included also is a remnant from past feminist literature, not introduced in any other of this controversy's works except the play—the concern over who is first cause in the sin of lust. Here also, as in the play, is an "Arraignment" of Joseph Swetnam himself.

She opens her pamphlet with a dedication to "All Right Honorable, Noble, and worthy Ladies" (A2). Her second dedicatory letter to "All Worthy and Hopefull young youths" contrasts with Swetnam's dedication to "giddy headed" youth. She says that she is not addressing the multitude. Swetnam's very assumption that his advice is necessary because of the pitfalls awaiting the young, most of whom are foolish, contrasts with both Tuvil's and Sowernam's dismissal of "giddy" youth as unworthy; she concerns herself with the "worthy Apprentices of London" who are above the common.

Chapters one and two are devoted to refuting, in conventional terms, some of Swetnam's conventional allegations. If woman is "crooked of conditions" because she was made of the crooked rib, remember that *"Joseph Swetnam* was made as from *Adam* of clay and dust, so he is of a durty and muddy disposition." And if "That which giueth quality to a thing, doth more abound in that quality; as fire which heateth, is it selfe more hot," then men must "excell in crookednesse" (13). In chapter two she describes the *"excellent prerogatiues God hath bestowed vpon Women."* Eve was the last created and therefore the best creation (5); she was created of a refined substance near man's heart and therefore was meant to be most dear to man; she is "commanded to obey her husband . . . the more to increase her glory. Obedience is better than Sacrifice: for nothing is more acceptable before God then to obey: Women are much bound to God, to haue so acceptable a vertue enioyned them for their pennance" (9-10). Chapters three and four are dedicated to stories of great women of the Bible: among others, Rebecca, Deborah, Judith, Ester, and Mary. Chapter five (marked iiii) includes stories of great women of *"ancient* and *former* times" (17).

The "arraignment" of Swetnam himself is the subject of chapters six, seven, and eight (marked v, vi, and vii). Chapter seven, his indictment, states briefly that he was accused of maligning all women although his pamphlet maintained that it would arraign only "lewde, idle, froward and vnconstant women" (29). He pleaded not guilty, we are told, but "being asked how hee would be tried, he stood mute." The women then considered "if we should haue vrged him to be pressed" (30), but decided that they would later be accused falsely of being unfair because most of those present were "of the fœminine gender." They then decided "to graunt him longer time to aduice with himselfe whether he would put himselfe to triall, or vpon better deliberation to recall his errours" (31).

Chapter eight then continues with further arguments in favor of women and against men: the devil took the shape of a man (33); women do not, as men do, fall in love with the opposite sex "for their apparell" (38). But, the most interesting consideration is whether woman or man is "first cause" in error: "*Helen* was the cause of *Troyes* burning; first, *Paris* did sollicite her; next, how many knaues and fooles of the male kinde had *Troy,* which to maintaine whoredome would bring their Citie to confusion" (46). And, "As *Eue* did not offend without the temptation of a Serpent; so women doe seldome offend, but it is by prouocation of men" (46-47). The treatise closes with a poem, signed by "Joane Sharp," of rhymed couplets which summarize the major arguments against, and condemnation of, Swetnam and his pamphlet.

The last direct answer to Swetnam before the play, Constantia Munda's *The Worming of a mad Dogge,* is similar to *Ester hath hang'd Haman* in that it is also feminist, as opposed to simply anti-Swetnam, and is likewise not specifically directed to the "common" people. It does, however, with Ester Sowernam's pamphlet, concede that there are *some* bad women, and imply that these are in the minority. It differs from all the works concerned in the controversey in that it comments, as well, on the times, specifically on the state of the publishing business and the theater. Constantia Munda's major contribution to the case against Swetnam are her criticism of his writing and education and her proposal that he thinks so little of women because he is the kind of man who frequents the places where low women can be found.

She notes, in an introductory poem, that Swetnam's "shameles muse" is so bad that it had nothing better to do than "fill/The itching eares of silly swaines" with "poyson'd drops of hemlocke" and "please/ The giddy headed vulgar" (A4-A4^V). The body of her pamphlet, invective liberally sprinkled with Latin and Greek, begins with a denunciation of the "many sottish and illiterate libels" and "sordid inuentions" which are "oppressing the presse" (1). She laments further: "When *scribimus indocti* must be the motto of everyone that fooles himselfe in Print: tis ridiculous! but when *scribimus insani* should be the signature of euery page, tis lamentable of our times" (2). Woman is "the most absolute worke composed by the worlds great Architect" (2-3) and a "neuer sufficiently glorified creation," and "Yet woman the greatest part of the *lesser world* is generally become the subiect of euery pendanticall goose-quill. Euery fantasticke Poetaster . . . will striue to represent vnseemly figments imputed to our sex, (as a pleasing theme to the vulgar) on the publique

Theatre" (3). Such persons who "gore the name and reputation of the innocent" should be put in shackles (3-4).

She attacks Swetnam himself, theorizing as to his reasons for attacking women. He blames all women for the faults of probably one who "hath giuen you as good as you brought." Just "Because you haue been guld with brasse money, will you thinke no cojne currant" (8). No matter his circumstances, he has no excuse: even "a pelting iniurie should not prouoke an approbrious calumnie" (8-9).

Swetnam's writing itself draws comment. He has copied, she says, the worst of bad writers: "let euery bird take his owne feather, and you would be as naked as Æsops iey" (22). She quotes from the *Araignment* and condemns his repetition of childish images: "Is it not irksome to a wise and discreet iudgement, to heare a booke stuft with such like sense as this, *The world is not made of oatmeale?*" She has heard some say it is made of atoms, none say oatmeal. "Sometimes you make me burst out with laughter" (23). She attacks his logic, and claims Swetnam's books should be burned for his own sake so that his ignorance will not be "blazoned abroad . . . to further ages" (26-27): he misquotes the *Bible,* Socrates, Plato, and Aristotle. Constantia Munda closes as Ester Sowernam does, with the statement that women mercifully wish him no bodily harm, such as should befall offenders, but, "these our writings shall be worse then fiers to torture both thy booke and thee" (34). There is no evidence, however, that any of these defenses bothered Swetnam much.

Two important generalizations must be made about the difference between the *Araignment* and the four pamphlets which answer it. First, none of Swetnam's adversaries appeals as directly as he does to the middle class—or, perhaps more properly, the "popular" reading audience. Daniel Tuvil, Rachel Speght, and Ester Sowernam all at least pretend to place themselves above the multitude by addressing their works to the learned and "honorable" ladies and gentlemen; Constantia Munda, besides addressing the upper classes, condemns the popular press. All four make much of learning—the three women, especially Constantia Munda, commenting on Swetnam's general lack of education. Although the weight of respectability—even logic—may have been on the side of the women's defenders, the general tone assumed by the four authors of the educated classes might not be expected to impress greatly the populace, more familiar with its prejudice than with the voice of reason. The popularity of the *Araignment,* far greater than that of any of its detractors, seems understandable because of its general tone and attitude alone.

This attitude on the part of those answering Swetnam, however, should not mislead us into believing that they really were directing their answers to a different audience. They were not of course. The statements imply, as all such statements do, that people of good sense will agree and that others will not. Such is the psychology of defense. And it is as expected a tactic as Swetnam's "between us common folk" appeal.

Secondly, one notes that the question of feminism, as opposed to equality of the sexes, is the concern really of only two of the answers, *Ester hath hang'd Haman* and *The Worming of a mad Dogge;* and even in these there are signs that less than feminine superiority might be a concession acceptable to the two authors. Ester Sowernam makes it clear that her grievance is based, at least in part, on Swetnam's condemnation of all women instead of just "bad" women; Constantia Munda is obviously as concerned with the abuses of the press and the stage of the time as the place of woman in current society. It is the play, however, which best reflects the attitude, which we shall call moderate, that is implied in the controversy and stated in Tuvil's pamphlet.

III.

A more likely title for *Swetnam the Woman-hater* would be *Lisandro and Leonida,* the names of the noble lovers whose story is the main plot. We are faced with the division of main plot and title plot. The title plot is concerned with Swetnam's (Misogenos') adventures in Sicily after his flight from England: he, with his clown companion Swash, distributes copies of his pamphlet; sets up a fencing school; volunteers to be the advocate for men in a debate commanded by the king to determine who is first cause in sin, man or woman; wins for his side; and, finally, is punished by the women for being what they consider the major cause of a tragedy that at the time is assumed accomplished. This tragedy or near tragedy is the subject of the main plot, the story based on a Juan de Flores "novelette."[15] The king, mourning the supposed loss of his only surviving son, assigns custody of his daughter, Leonida, to Nicanor, a lord who covets the throne and hopes to gain it either through marriage to the princess or through disposal of both her and her father. The princess, however, is in love with a Prince Lisandro, with whom she is caught in apparently compromising circumstances; she is sentenced to death and he is exiled, after the debate to determine who is "first cause." Through the plotting and manipulations of Lorenzo (the young prince who has not died but has returned to the court in disguise), Queen Aurelia, and the loyal Lord Iago, both Leonida and Lisandro (who had attempted suicide because of the princess' apparent death) are saved, and King Atticus, who sentenced them, repents his hasty decision. The villain, Nicanor, also repents, and all ends happily. The two plots come together at the debate, which is meant to determine the fates of the prince and princess. The prologue and epilogue are concerned with Swetnam's activities, but the action proper opens and closes with the Princess Leonida-Prince Lisandro story.

Professor Matulka says that the play "serves as a strong feministic document, while at the same time it attacks one of the most notorious women-haters of the period in England."[16] She overstates the play's feminist inclinations, trying too hard to make similar the situations under which the tragi-comedy and Juan de Flores' tragedy were written. Juan de Flores was a feminist, and his story is feminist; *Swetnam the Woman-hater* is not. In spite of some excesses in statement and extremes in characterization which might lead one to believe that the play is a feminist work, it actually assumes a neutral position. Perhaps the most accurate description of its overall view is that in Iago's speech,

> And to say the truth,
> Both Sexes equally should beare the blame;
> For both offend alike. (IV, i, 11-13)

and in Scanfardo's statement to Misogenos following one of the latter's anti-feminist tirades.

> Me thinks you are too generall: some, no doubt,
> As many men, are bad: condemne not all for some. (I, ii, 161-162)

The most obvious revelation of this attitude appears in the playwright's handling of the debate (who is the "first agent" in affairs of love, man or woman?) between Misogenos and Lorenzo, disguised as the Amazon, Atlanta. One is tempted to cite the debate itself as primary evidence of the playwright's attitude of moderation. No one really wins the argument, although Misogenos (and therefore men) wins the judgment. The case for neither side is strong enough to sway a really impartial jury, as an Elizabethan, or almost any other audience, would admit.

Each advocate presents first a clever, but conventional argument: Atlanta points out that one cannot blame the wax for the imprint made in it; women cannot be blamed as "first agent," because

> Lust tempteth Beautie:
> Witnesse the vowes, the oaths, the protestations,
> And Crocodile teares of base dissembling men,
> To winne their shamelesse purpose: (III, iii, 100-104)

Misogenos counters by pointing out that, as "A Citie Tradesman" is aware that "the garish setting out/ Of Beautie in their shops will call in Customers" (III, iii, 154-157) so women understand "The mysterie of Painting, Curling, Powdring" (III, iii, 176). And then the debate closes with Misogenos recalling historically good men and bad women, and Atlanta countering with historically good women and bad men. Obviously, neither argument is conclusive.

Misogenos, however, is somewhat the cleverer of the two. It would be difficult to say that Lorenzo does an excellent job "in defence/ Of wronged women" (III, iii, 137). He is intemperate throughout almost all of his argument following the "exordium." And, near the finish of the trial, when he loses his temper to the point of abandoning the argument per se to insult Misogenos, that "Base snarling Dogge" (III, iii, 207), the woman-hater cleverly comes back with "O doe not scold, good woman!" (215). Atlanta has to admit, "I forgot my selfe" (216), showing, in the judges' eyes at least, one of woman's weaknesses. However, the audience cannot forget the obvious: this intemperate scolding advocate for the women is not a woman, but Lorenzo in disguise; the playwright's ironic point is well made. The judgment is also in question because, as Atlanta says to the judges,

> You are all men, and in this weightie businesse,
> Graue Women should haue sate as Iudges with you.   (III, iii, 264-265)

The debate aside, however, the audience knows that the fault lies with both Lisandro and Leonida, although one's first inclination is to cite the former as the "first agent." It is, after all, he who dons Friar Anthonie's habit to gain forbidden access to Leonida's quarters. And, one might argue, he pays no heed to Leonida's letter requesting that he leave her. However, a closer look at this scene, involving Loretta, Lisandro, and Leonida's letter, reveals that to judge only Lisandro guilty would be somewhat unfair. Loretta tells him that

> shee prayes you, henceforth to desist,
> Respecting your owne safetie: Worthie Prince,
> The times are troublesome and dangerous:

but then adds,

> As for her selfe, she's arm'd to vndergoe
> All malice that for you they can inflict.   (II, i, 17-21)

One is tempted, certainly, to agree with Lisandro when he reads Leonida's letter and observes,

> See what a negatiue command shee hath
> Impos'd vpon my sloth to visit her,
> As if she taxed my neglect so long: (II, i, 35-37)

The play seems to say subtly that Lisandro's action is prompted, somewhat at least, by Leonida's letter. He does not mention, at any rate, a plan to see her until he has read her message. One also wonders how seriously we may take previous mentions of Leonida's character as we interpret this scene. There is, surely, question as to how favorable the previous descriptions of her are meant to be. Her beauty is certain: Iago and Atticus both mention this, and the number and favor of her suitors are testimony enough to her physical charm. However, her father describes her as "wanton, coy, and fickle" (I, i, 162) and Iago says she has treated the loves of Italian princes "with contempt and crueltie" (I, iii, 48). And these are the voices of friendly criticism. If one sees any validity in these hints about Leonida's character, we can easily assume that she is not about to dismiss her real love, Lisandro, as easily as the superficial content of her message through Loretta states. The implications seem far too important to ignore.

Lastly, here, we must remember that, no matter the motives of the lovers, the debate is made necessary in the first place because each assumes the guilt for the other's actions. The protestations of both Lisandro and Leonida make it impossible for the audience to decide, without prejudice, who is most at fault.

A second consideration which seems to reflect the play's attitude toward the general issue of who is superior, man or woman, is what might be called the balance of characters. For such a purpose, one may simplify matters greatly, without harming the play, by classifying the characters simply as "good" and "evil." For this two-part division, the main characters in the "good" category are Lorenzo, Lisandro, Leonida, Loretta, and Iago. All of these—excepting, possibly, Lorenzo, who tends to be overly zealous in his affection for the female sex—incline toward a neutral stand in the argument. Lisandro and Leonida are both equally noble and ignoble, though the "ignoble" label may be inappropriate, since we are led to believe that Leonida ended her clandestine evening with Lisandro as chaste as she began it. Lorenzo, who is an obvious representation of the equality of the sexes in at least one way—he, the noble prince, appears before all in the guise of Atlanta, the noble amazon—is the undisputed hero of the play. Iago, the good and loyal prince, states his belief that blame lies equally. Loretta, not a perfect young lady, by any means, since she does believe that she has a right to do anything—good or bad—if her betters precede her, is loyal and honest to her mistress and to her lover, Scanfardo. And she, in spite of her deviousness, can never be blamed for dishonesty.

Misogenos, the woman-hater, in balance with Lorenzo, is the obvious villain, along with Nicanor, who balances the good Iago. Scanfardo is the dishonest and villainous counterpart to Loretta. Lisandro and Leonida, not representing good balanced with bad, are equals, more importantly in guilt than in social class, and so are Atticus and Aurelia, although the latter are less important to the man-woman question.

A most interesting aspect of *Swetnam* is its subtle comment on the man-woman controversy through the attitudes and actions of its characters. This comment is less obvious than the direct statements made through the balance of "good" and "evil" characters or the formal argument between Atlanta and Misogenos, a debate which proves nothing except that there is something (or nothing) to say for both sides. Amusing ironies occur in the play, most of which are concerned with a character's attribution of his own weaknesses to others; for example, Nicanor, who wishes to marry Leonida primarily to assure himself the kingdom when Atticus dies, tells us that "nothing batters more/ A womans resolution, then rich gifts" (II, i, 108-109). In the same speech he says that he will not give up just because Leonida rebuffs him:

> . . . No Citie
> Euer yeelded at first skirmish. Before,
> You came but to a parley, thou shalt now
> Giue an assault: . . .   (II, i, 105-108)

This sounds much like an argument which Lisandro will use later when he tries to protect Leonida:

> For what can Women aboue weakenesse act?
> Or, what Fort's so strong, but yeelds at length
> To a continued siege?   (III, i, 63-65)

We cannot help but note that Nicanor's very actions seem to support the argument that men are the first cause of fault.

It is, however, a scene between Scanfardo and Loretta, the two servants, that is most humorous and ironic. Here the roles usually attributed to the sexes are reversed. Loretta knows the secret of Lisandro's and Leonida's meeting, and Scanfardo peevishly will not rest until he finds it out. We have, in a sense, a comic parallel to — even a parody of — Shakespeare's scene between Brutus and Portia in *Julius Caesar*. Scanfardo notes that "there's something in the wind," but Loretta assures him that there is "Nothing indeed." Finally, Scanfardo, woman-like, sulks, "Dare you not trust me?" When Loretta says she will tell him, she delivers the most ironic line of all, "But as you are a man reueale it not." Scanfardo's reaction, one usually reserved for women in these circumstances, is anger that she should mistrust him, her lover. Of course he cannot be trusted; he will betray her mistress to Nicanor. And, after she leaves to await his arrival in bed, he observes:

> What will not women blab to those they loue?
> I am very loth to leaue my sport tonight,
> And yet more loth to lose that rich reward
> My Lord will giue for this discouerie. (II, ii, 156-159).

Thus we have the man behaving like a curious woman, trying to find out what is none of his business, and the woman in the role of a traditional naive man, trusting her lover and betraying both herself and her mistress.

Another somewhat amusing reflection of the playwright's neutral stand is seen in the relationship between Atticus and Aurelia. At first glance Atticus appears to be a combination of the desirable and undesirable; and Aurelia seems a flatter character because she is simply on the side of mercy, as Atticus is not, and among those opposed to Swetnam, who is never sympathetic. However, a more careful consideration will show that Aurelia, like Atticus, always has our sympathy, although we cannot always approve of her actions. One of the subtlest comments on the relationship between man and woman comes as an almost humorous element in one of the least humorous scenes. After the apparent execution of Leonida and suicide of Lisandro, Atticus receives a report from Iago on how events passed. He is greatly disturbed by the fact that his daughter went to her death saying she was "free'd of Fathers tyrannie" (V, i, 52). Obviously he is beginning to have doubts about his previous decision. Although these events are his fault, we cannot escape a sympathetic response (such as we feel for Lear or for any other such character), especially as we watch his own reaction which seems to predict an emotional breakdown. In the midst of this most disturbing scene, Aurelia enters to berate him. She calls him tyrannical and cruel. She curses him. She wounds him most acutely, perhaps, by pointing out his obvious flaw — a compulsion to put his desire for fame as a just king above his obligation to act mercifully and to use due deliberation. When Atticus attempts to get away from her, she follows, like a fury, even as he rushes off stage.

> Goe where thou wilt, still will I follow thee,
> And with my sad laments still beat thy eares,
> Till all the world of thy iustice heares. (V, i, 108-110)

If it were not for the seriousness of the scene, one would be reminded of the nagging wife who had been a subject for English humor since medieval times.

Other results of the dramatist's effort to lessen the severity of the man-woman argument appear in the scene of Swetnam's arraignment. In the first place the levity of this episode in which Swetnam is punished by women contrasts vividly with the cruelty shown by the women in the novelette on which the play is based. In the second place, one notes in this scene which belongs to the women, humorous lines at their expense. Swash, brought back to the place of the trial after attempting escape, explains,

> I could not find the way out of the Orchard,
> If I should ha' beene hang'd, but fell into these
> Old Women's mouthes: but the best is, They had
> No teeth to bite me, but my Grandame here
> Scratches most deuillishly. (V, ii, 189-193)

And later, when asked by Aurelia if he ever loved a woman, the clown answers, "I, with all my heart" (213), and Scold comments, "He lookes as if he did" (213). Even Misogenos' reaction to his sentence prevents our taking the scene and the general question too seriously. He shall be

> ... bayted by all the honest women in the Parish.
> *Misog.* Is that the worst? there will not one be found
> In all the Citie. (V, ii, 334-336)

In the entire play only two elements possibly contribute to an interpretation that *Swetnam the Woman-hater* is feminist. The first, based on the activity of Misogenos, carries little weight, since the woman-hater is meant throughout to be a comic object of scorn and cannot be taken to represent men in general. The circumstances of his falling in love provide an obvious comment in favor of women. Misogenos is guilty of the very actions of which Atlanta accuses men: When he falls in love with the amazon (Lorenzo), he claims to be in great agony. He sends a letter to Atlanta which professes his love in extravagant terms, described as "The very quintessence of flatterie" (IV, v, 151). Once he receives a favorable answer, the prize no longer seems as valuable. Fickle as any woman could be, he now says that any past talk of love "were a iest indeed" (V, ii, 81).

Lorenzo presents the strongest evidence for a feminist interpretation and that evidence is weakened by contradictory statements such as his agreement, during the debate, that

> In all their passions women are impetuous,
> And beyond men, ten times more violent. (III, iii, 92-93)

His praise, at least once, is extreme. After hearing Misogenos' tirade against women, he tells Iago,

18 Swetnam the Woman-hater

> I will not see the glories of that Sexe
> Be-spawld by such a dogged Humorist,
> And passe vnpunisht.   (III, ii, 51-53)

When Iago asks what he intends to do, Lorenzo answers,

> To vndertake this iust and honest quarrell,
> In the defence of Vertue, till I haue
> Seuerely punisht his opprobrious word,
> Committed against Women, who's iust fame
> Merits an Angels Pen to register.   (54-58)

Later in the scene, accepting the challenge as defender of women, he is milder, if still feminist.

> What woman can indure to heare the Wrongs
> Slanders, Reproches, and base Forgeries,
> That baser men vaunt forth, to dimme the rayes
> Of our weake tender Sex? But they shall know,
> Themselues, not women, are the cause of woe.   (139-143)

This claim, however, must be considered in light of the preceding assertion of women's guilt by Misogenos and the heralding of him by the men as their "champion." It is also true, as we have discussed earlier, that Lorenzo's zeal, specifically in the debate, will do more harm than good for woman's cause. Even if one assumes that Lorenzo is a serious representative of the feminist point of view, one must admit that that point of view does not come off very well.

Finally, the seriousness with which the playwright could take any argument other than one for equality of the sexes is perhaps best reflected in the purpose of the play. In spite of the importance of the Swetnam plot and the great amount of space devoted to it in the play, the major concern of *Swetnam the Woman-hater* does not seem to be the man-woman question. At least equally important are the questions brought up by Atticus' misinterpretation of justice, his inability to recognize which was friendly and which was unfriendly counsel (the traditional error of mistaking criticism for disloyalty, flattery for sincerity), and the attempts of both Atticus and Nicanor to force Leonida to love a man other than one of her own choice. And, of course, we must finally admit that the play's real purpose, above all, was to entertain the Red Bull audience for whom it was written.

Here we come to a consideration that is among the strongest in the argument that *Swetnam the Woman-hater* reflects an attitude that was generally acceptable to at least many, if not the majority, of the common people of the time. The play was performed by Queen Anne's players probably before the Queen's death, March 2, 1619, at the Red Bull Theater. The Red Bull audience, as we know, was a "commoner" audience. It is unlikely that the playwright of *Swetnam the Woman-hater,* who had put into his play so many other elements designed to appeal to this kind of audience,[17] would have expressed a sentiment toward women that would have been generally unpopular. Gerald E. Bentley proffers a judgment that, if sound, further supports the opinion that the sentiment of the play corresponded closely with the sentiments of the audience. Discussing the scene in which Swetnam is "arraigned," he says, "the popularity of this part of the play is indicated not only by the prologue and epilogue, but by the preparation of a cut of the scene for the title-page."[18]

Perhaps the safest conclusion to draw from the preceding discussion is that the audience of the "popular" stage preferred entertainment in its theater and was less concerned with the inherent superiority of man over woman or woman over man than with having fun. However, the very fact that this audience could have fun at such great expense to Swetnam, the notorious woman-hater, hints that it probably did not take his views very seriously. And, the fact that it was not offered a piece in praise of woman's superiority hints that it probably could not take that position very seriously, either. Indeed, it is the implicit assumption of the play (i.e., that only a fool would suggest one extreme or the other) that finally seems most important.

Notes

1. *The Araignment Of Lewde, idle, froward, and vnconstant women: Or the vanitie of them, choose you whether. With a Commendacion of wise, vertuous and honest Women. Pleasant for married Men, profitable for young Men, and hurtfull to None.* (1615). Hereafter cited as the *Araignment*.

2. For a complete title-page description see the end of "A Note on the Text."

3. Joseph Swetnam, *The Schoole of the Noble and Worthy Science of Defence. Being the first of any English-mans inuention, which professed the sayd Science; So plainly described, that any man may quickly come to the true knowledge of their weapons, with small paines and little practise. Then reade it advisedly, and vse the benefit thereof when occasion shal serue, so shalt thou be a good Common-wealth man, liue happy to thy selfe, and comfortable to thy friend. Also many other good and profitable Precepts and Counsels for the managing of Quarrels and ordering thy selfe in many other matters.* (London, 1617). Hereafter cited as the *Schoole*.

4. Alexander B. Grosart, "Swetnam the Woman-hater," with notes, illustrations and facsimiles, *Occasional Issues,* XIV (Manchester, 1880). Only 62 copies were printed.

5. Barbara Matulka, *The Novels of Juan De Flores and Their European Diffusion* (New York, 1931).

6. Louis B. Wright, *Middle-Class Culture in Elizabethan England* (Chapel Hill, 1935), p. 507.

7. The *STC* lists ten editions before 1634; following that date, editions appeared in 1690, 1702, 1707, 1733, and 1807. There were also translations into Dutch published in 1641 and 1645.

8. Wright, p. 506.

9. *Asylum Veneris, or A Sanctuary for Ladies. Iustly Protecting them, their virtues, and sufficiencies from the foule aspersions and forged imputations of traducing Spirits* (1616). Hereafter cited as *Asylum Veneris*.

10. *A Mouzell for Melastomus, The Cynicall Bayter of, and foule mouthed Barker against Evahs Sex. Or an Apologeticall Answere to that Irreligious and Illiterate Pamphlet made by Io. Sw. and by him Intituled, The Arraignement of Women* (1617). Hereafter cited as *A Mouzell for Melastomus*.

11. *Ester hath hang'd Haman: or An Answere to a lewd Pamphlet, entituled, The Arraignment of Women. With the arraignment of lewd, idle,*

froward, and vnconstant men, and Husbands (1617). Hereafter cited as *Ester hath hang'd Haman.*

12. *The Worming of a mad Dogge: or, A Soppe For Cerberus The Iaylor of Hell. No Confutation But a sharpe Redargution of the baytor of Women* (1617). Hereafter cited as *The Worming of a mad Dogge.*

13. Grosart, viii.

14. Tuvil says in his introduction that he is publishing his work, which he wrote earlier, only because there is danger that "some imperfect copies" may be published. Wright, p. 488, says that "apparently the pressure from printers for works about women was too much for him to resist." He also notes that the *DNB* lists *Asylum Veneris* as part of the controversy. Charles Carroll Camden in *The Elizabethan Woman* (Houston, 1952), p. 255, maintains that "the popularity of Swetnam's diatribe" would make it seem "likely that Tuvil's . . . publication, if not an exact reply, was at least intended to capitalize on the popular interest."

15. The plot is based on the story of *Aurelio and Isabel,* the English version of the *Historia de Aurelio e Isabella,* a translated version of a Spanish work, *Grisel Y Mirabella* by Juan de Flores. For a more complete discussion of the relationship between the play and its source, see chapter 2, part I.

16. Matulka, p. 220.

17. On the nature of the Red Bull audience, see Gerald E. Bentley, *The Jacobean and Caroline Stage,* 5 vols. (Oxford, 1941-56), vol. i, p. 165ff., and George F. Reynolds, *The Staging of Elizabethan Plays at the Red Bull Theater 1605-1625* (London, 1940), pp. 7-9.

18. Bentley, v, 1417.

Chapter 2.

Source, Stage History, and Authorship

I.

Gerard Langbaine was the first to record the source of *Swetnam the Woman-hater* as a "novelette" attributable to Juan de Flores.[1] The play was derived from the *Historia de Aurelio e Isabella,* a translated and slightly modified version of a Spanish and apparently superior work, *Grisel Y Mirabella,* by the fifteenth century writer, Juan de Flores. He is described as "a Castilian noble" who was "A Chivalrous defender of woman."[2] The playwright's debt to this novelette is noted by the Rev. Mr. Grosart in his 1880 edition and discussed thoroughly by Barbara Matulka, a scholar of Spanish and comparative literature, in her study of the European influence of Juan de Flores. Professor Matulka calls *Grisel Y Mirabella,* written about 1495,[3] "a combative feminist story, which became a ladies' Bible and a courtiers' manual."[4] It was not *Grisel Y Mirabella,* however, but *Aurelio e Isabella* which was well known and influential on the continent, itself translated into French, back into Spanish, and finally into English.[5] Five editions were published in English before *Swetnam the Woman-hater* was staged, all multilingual printings designed as language teaching aids. Two in 1556, one in 1588, and another in 1608 were four-language editions—Italian, Spanish, French and English set in columns side by side. The fifth was a three-language edition (French, Italian, and English) in 1586.[6]

The story of *Aurelio and Isabel* differs from *Grisel Y Mirabella* in no way significant to consideration of the former as the source of *Swetnam the Woman-hater.* The most obvious change is in the names. The lovers, Grisel and Mirabella, become Aurelio and Isabel; Bracayda, the defender of her sex's reputation, becomes Hortensia; and Torrellas, the woman hater, becomes Afranio.[7]

The story is set in Scotland where the king, who has but one child, the beautiful Isabel, has neglected to arrange or approve a marriage, although his daughter is past the age that requires it; he believes no one in Scotland worthy of her and has rejected all previous suitors. Because Isabel is so beautiful that many men have died for her love after little more than a glance, the king orders her put away in a place "secret ynoughe" where no one can see her.

However, when Isabel learns of the knight Aurelio's great love for her, she, in turn, falls in love with him. Aurelio gains access to her room where they consummate their love and continue to meet in secret, the only one aware of the meetings being an old gentlewoman who has free access to Isabel's quarters. She finally betrays the secret to one of the king's stewards with whom she is in love; he in turn tells the king. The father catches the two in bed. The ensuing fight concludes with the capture of Aurelio and the imprisonment of the lovers. The guilty pair are then brought before the judges, who must decide which of the two is most at fault; for, in the story, under Scottish law, the greater offender must burn at the stake and the second must suffer banishment.

Aurelio and Isabel both claim to be the instigator, each trying to save the other's life. The judges decide that they are equally guilty, but because the king prides himself on being just, and the law has to be satisfied—daughter or no—they suggest that advocates for each sex be found to argue, in front of impartial judges, who is the first cause in such crimes, men or women. The advocates are Hortensia, a wise and discreet defender of women, and Afranio, a notorious woman hater. Much of the novelette is devoted to their debate.

Hortensia argues that men use all kinds of devices to attract women, and that women have little choice but to give in, since, as a last resort, a man may lie to ruin the woman's reputation and to save his own pride. Afranio counters that men deceive women and pursue them, but women never repulse these advances; in fact they encourage them, sometimes using wiles far more effective than words. But, says Hortensia, men—who are more learned and experienced—should set good examples for women; but instead, they act so pitifully with their declarations and protestations that women, moved by mercy, give in. Women, Afranio answers, deck themselves out in clothes and jewels, making themselves more beautiful than nature meant them to be, to tempt men. Both parties call on history for examples of good and bad women to support their arguments. At the debate's close, the judges—all men—award the victory to Afranio; the women protest, citing the natural prejudice of the judges. Isabel is to burn, and Aurelio is to watch as part of his punishment; then he is to be banished.

When the lovers are brought forth for the execution, Aurelio leaps into the flames before the Princess can be put to death and thereby saves her from the stake: one life is all that is demanded for the crime. The princess, in despair, joins her lover in death by leaping from a castle room and being eaten by the king's lions.

The queen and Hortensia swear to avenge these deaths on Afranio, who plays into their hands by falling in love with Hortensia. He sends her a letter professing love and declaring repentance for what he has said against women. Hortensia decides to encourage him in order to get him alone so that the women can carry out their revenge. She answers his letter, arranging for a secret meeting in the palace; and he, believing he has made an easy conquest and at the same time proved the truth of his charges made against women in the debate, pridefully shows the letter to other men and mocks women all the more.

When he appears for the assignation with Hortensia, he is greeted first by her alone; but after an initial encouragement, the queen and many women rush in. He is stripped, tied to a post, and tortured by each of the women. When he is almost dead, they feast in the same room and jeer at him, so as to make the torture last as long as possible. When he is dead, his body is burned, and each of the ladies takes some of his ashes as a memento; they will long have the pleasure of recalling their vengeance on the woman-hater. The parallels to the plot of *Swetnam* are as obvious as the major difference in tone between the two. The novel takes the anti-feminist phenomenon more seriously than does the play.

Let us consider the characters. The Scottish king, like Atticus of *Swetnam the Woman-hater,* is proud of his reputation as a just king, and this pride leads them both to excessive severity with their daughters. Both daughters are so beautiful that they have caused the deaths of previous suitors, but both, once they have committed themselves, remain ardently loyal to their lovers. Both are thought to be the sole surviving children of their parents, and marriage in both cases will apparently decide the future rulers of the kingdoms. Aurelio and Lisandro are similarly faithful and devoted lovers. The two queens are driven by similar desires to save their daughters from what they feel is the tyranny of their husbands. Atlanta and Hortensia play comparable roles, and although Atlanta is really Lorenzo in disguise, she is as esteemed by the women she defends as is Hortensia, a real female. Loretta, Leonida's gentlewoman, and her lover, Scanfardo, can be compared to the gentlewoman and the steward of the novelette, the couples through which the lovers of both stories are found out. The functions of these characters are alike, although the gentlewoman and steward are not really important as characters in themselves; Loretta and Scanfardo, especially the former, are more fully developed.

It is, however, in plot that the stories are most similar: the kingdoms' laws are the same; both daughters are imprisoned for similar reasons; both are caught in similar crimes (although we are led to believe Leonida is still chaste, appearances aside); both sets of lovers partake in a "combat of generosity" which leads to similar sentences. The revenge of the women on the male advocates in both cases results from the advocate's falling in love with his adversary; and the plots for revenge are carried out alike. The complaints of the women (i.e., that the jury is entirely male) following the judgment are the same. The major difference is that the novelette is "tragic" and the play is "comic": Misogenos is a fool; his actions are mostly comic. The difference between Swetnam and Afranio is well exemplified by the difference between their falling in love: Hortensia is, besides an intelligent and talented debater, a beautiful woman; Swetnam falls in love with what the audience knows is a man and what Swash, who believes the the female identity, describes as "A Masculine Feminine" (IV, iii, 65).

Even when he is "arraigned" by the women, his plight is comic; his torture is mostly by fingernail and tooth, and does not result in his death. In fact, no deaths at all occur in *Swetnam the Woman-hater*. One might speculate that the playwright deliberately adapted the story to the tragi-comic form because he could not justify the severity of Afranio's treatment in *Aurelio and Isabel*. One reason for the difference in treatment could stem from the reality of Joseph Swetnam; there was no living, breathing Afranio to feel sorry for.

It may be interesting here to note one of the ironies involved in the adaptation of Afranio's character for Swetnam, the adaptation of a fictitious for a real person. Torrellas, Juan de Flores' woman-hater, was modeled after a real person, and, when Lelio Aletiphilo, the novelette's adapter, changed Torrellas' name to Afranio, Professor Matulka says, much of the effectiveness of the character was lost, "the historical background was effaced." The name Torrellas meant something to the Spanish reader: "the arguments of Torrellas . . . were but sign posts and indications . . . of what he knew of Torrellas' satires." And, because this reference is not there in the Italian version, it is "difficult to accept and justify Afranio's torture and murder, whereas the Spanish reader, if severely inclined and remembering the violences of the Spanish feminist quarrel, could agree that no punishment was too dire for the vicious slanders of Torrellas and his kin."[8] The name Swetnam, of course, meant something to the English reader; but whereas Torrellas was a respectable, and by many an esteemed literary personality, there is no reason to believe that Joseph Swetnam was anywhere near as imposing. Here again is evidence that Professor Matulka misleads us in likening the situations under which the Juan de Flores work and the play were written; here also is further reason to believe that Swetnam's contemporaries did not take him very seriously.

To look at the arguments used by the debaters in both the novelette and the play would show further parallels, but there is a danger here, one that results from the nature of the feminist debate itself. Professor Matulka says, when she discusses the arguments as they appear in the Juan de Flores work:

> An attempt to trace the source of the arguments in the feminist debate in the *Grisel y Mirabella* would merely result in an almost infinite duplication of parallels, each of which may, or may not, have inspired Juan de Flores. If the numerous opponents of women in all their bitterness hardly ever evolved a single original argument, their champions were equally and sadly impersonal in whatever they said to the glory of womanly honor.[9]

Finally, there are two further similarities, both concerned with character names. The first makes rather tenuous evidence: the apparent borrowing of the name, Aurelio, from the prose work, for Aurelia, the queen, in the play. This, however, is the only name borrowed, and it moves from the young male lover to the older female. More substantial evidence, strangely enough not noted by the Rev. Mr. Grosart, is the erroneous occurrence twice in the quarto of the name heading, *Hortensia*.[10] There is no textual explanation for the use of this name; it occurs nowhere else in the play. Apparently the playwright had the story of Aurelio and Isabel fresh in his mind; or, perhaps he had a copy of the novelette before him. However, it should be noted that in both places the name *Hortensia* occurs in place of *Leonida,* who is not the counterpart of the novelette's Hortensia, but of its Isabel. If the play were written with the novelette immediately before the playwright, we would be told, if nothing else, something about the author's method of composition, and possibly we should gain thereby a further clue to the authorship of the play. We shall reconsider the problem in the third section of this chapter.

II.

Swetnam the Woman-hater was probably first performed sometime in 1618 or 1619 by Queen Anne's players at the Red Bull theater. Since evidence from the play indicates that its composition followed publication of all the pamphlets, its production on the stage must have occurred after publication of Constantia Munda's *The Worming of a mad Dogge,* entered April 29, 1617, the last of the "answers" to Swetnam. Swash, during Misogenos' arraignment, in a passage cited before, says of his master,

> He put his Booke i' the Presse, and publisht it,
> And made a thousand men and wiues fall out.
> Till two or three good wenches, in meere spight,
>
> Laid their heads together, and rail'd him out of th' Land. (V, ii, 320-323)

Professor Bentley, citing this passage, says that the play "could not have appeared before late 1617," after the pamphlets were published, and ventures further that "spight" (322) may be meant as a pun on the last name of Rachel Speght, the author of *A Mouzell for Melastomus*,[11] entered on November 14, 1616. F. G. Fleay agrees only that it must have been written and performed between 1615 and Queen Anne's death, March 2, 1619;[12] George F. Reynolds, citing Felix Schelling, places the performance in 1618 or 1619;[13] and E. K. Chambers puts it before the Queen's death.[14]

Professor Matulka, noting that the title page mentions that the play was acted "by the late Queenes Seruants" suggests that "[s]ince Queen Anne died on March 2, 1619, and [the play was] licensed on October 17, 1619, the play must have been staged between these two dates."[15] Although the guess is an understandable one, we should admit the probability that the play was performed before Anne's death. The title page reference was composed for the play's publication in 1620. By this time, of course, the company was the *late* "Queenes Seruants"; it may have been simply "the Queenes Seruants" when *Swetnam the Womanhater* was performed. Professor Bentley says that "all the London theatres were closed and presumably remained closed until [the Queen's] ... funeral on 13 May 1619."[16] He and John T. Murray state that the company ceased to exist under Anne's name, although provincial companies continued for a time as "Servants to the Late Queen Anne."[17] By November, 1619 most of the company had dispersed, and the remainder probably had been given a patent as Players of the Revels.[18] It seems most likely then, that the play was performed in 1618, probably late in 1618, although there is no substantial evidence to support this likelihood. We have only the rather certain terminal dates, 1617 and 1619: it was written in 1617 or afterward and performed before the Queen's death.

There is evidence, according to Professor Bentley, that *Swetnam the Woman-hater* was performed at least a second time sometime around 1633: "About fifteen years after it was first performed Thomas Nabbes referred to it in his *Tottenham Court,* acted at the Salisbury Court theatre in 1633." The wife in the play refers to arraigning one of the other characters, "as one was in a play." She wishes to "aggravate his indictment to the Jury; which shall be Midwives of my acquaintance." In a later scene she says, "He is one into whom the spirit of *Swetnam's* crept. I hope sir you are of a kinder disposition to our sexe." Professor Bentley states, "These allusions, one of which certainly depends upon the familiarity of the Salisbury Court audience with the play, suggest that in 1633 it may have been recently performed, perhaps at the Salisbury Court."[19]

III.

The author of *Swetnam the Woman-hater* is not known, and attempts to identify him most likely must focus on internal evidence: no external record of the play's authorship has been found. Comparing the similarity of the themes and characters in the play with the themes and characters of known authors of the time will provide nothing conclusive because individual plays shared a great many of the same "stock" elements. We shall discuss many of these elements in chapter three.

The Rev. Mr. Grosart mentions in his introduction that some believe the playwright may be Thomas Dekker, and others prefer Thomas Heywood. (He does not, however, identify these persons.)[20] One fact which strengthens the candidacy of Dekker and Heywood is the association of both with the Red Bull at this time. There were other available writers, needless to say, and Professor Bentley mentions the possibility that some of the Red Bull plays were written by Thomas Drewe, an actor with the Queen's Men at the time. However, since evidence is notably lacking, supposition becomes hazardous; the writer Drewe, for example, may not have been the actor of the same name.[21]

Although the Rev. Mr. Grosart will not commit himself absolutely, he seems to favor the Heywood guess. He cites as very minor evidence a usage of "obdure" (II, i, 72) in *Swetnam the Woman-hater* which occurs twice in Heywood's *Golden Age*. He points to the following lines:

> Too pittilesse, and too *obdur's* the King,
> To cloyster beauty from the sight of men,

and

> Be deafe vnto her prayers, blinde to her teares,
> *Obdure* to her relenting passions.[22]

He does not mention the pertinence of the sentiment expressed by the first two lines to *Swetnam the Woman-hater*.

The major reason that the Heywood guess is so tempting seems to be the interest of the play in the feminist controversy and the kind of defense it presents. Professor Wright makes the strongest statement in favor of Heywood, but he also avoids declaring himself absolutely.

> *Swetnam the Woman-hater* is well written, in the manner of Thomas Heywood. The language, dialogue, and clownery are all patterned after Heywood, and the defense of women is precisely the sort of thing he might have written. It is not improbable that this may be one of the plays in which he had a "main finger."²³

This is not an unreasonable observation, in spite of the fact that there are many plays of the time which treat the feminine controversy, two of which, *Female Rebellion* and Fletcher's *The Sea Voyage,* Professor Wright mentions in the very note in which he suggests Heywood as a probable author of the play.²⁴

There are two other clues which could help to identify the author, but neither is so typically Heywood, as opposed to any other author, as to be conclusive. First there are reflections of Shakespearian scenes, characters, and themes in *Swetnam the Woman-hater* which might also point to Heywood, but again there are such reflections in much Jacobean drama. There is love between a boy and a girl of families which apparently do not get along: Atticus says Lisandro will not wed his daughter because, "His father and Our selfe were still at oddes" (I, i, 173). Lisandro attempts suicide over the body of Leonida who has been given something to make her appear dead. Atticus is an uncompromising king who allows his pride to reflect merciless severity as sense of duty. He echoes arguments heard in Shakespeare's authoritarians:

> Arise; and know, A King is like a Starre,
> By which each Subiect, as a Mariner,
> Must steere his course.   (III, iii, 276-278)

When asked to excuse the prince and princess and "impute" their crime "to their childish loue," he answers,

> To loue, my Lords? if that were lowable,
> What Act so vile, but might be so excus'd?
> The Murderer, that sheddeth guiltlesse bloud,
> Might plead, it was for loue of his Reuenge,
> The Felon likewise might excuse his theft,
> With loue of money, and the Traytor too
> Might say, It was for loue of Soueraigntie.   (III, i, 24-30)

Secondly, there is some reason to believe that the play was written with its source either immediately in front of the playwright or very fresh in his mind. Twice there are erroneous references in the quarto to the name of a character who does not appear in the play but who does appear in its source. The inclusion of these names in the quarto hints strongly that an author's copy of the play, perhaps a "fair copy" marked over by the bookkeeper, might have been the copy from which the quarto was set. There is also the possibility that the author composed the play originally using several names from *Aurelio and Isabel,* transferring the names to other characters in the play. Later, he revised the work, or a collaborator-reviser did so, removing the source names, perhaps wishing to imply that the play is primarily a play about Swetnam and not an adaptation of another story. In his apparent attempt to remove evidence that the play is a dramatization of the novella, he either overlooked Aurelio, or thought it sufficiently disguised as Aurelia, the queen and not Aurelio, the princess' lover. He missed the two occurrences of Hortensia, and thus, when the printer worked from the ms., he preserved these names in the printed version. There is the possibility that the quarto was not set from some kind of author's papers, that the ms. was a close copy of such papers and the scribe included the original errors. However, this possibility is even less probable than the speculation that author's papers were used.

Pertinent to the condition of the quarto and the projected condition of the ms. from which it was set is Heywood's reputation as a fast and competent, if not highly gifted, writer. W. W. Greg notes that a writer such as Heywood "who boasted having had at least a main finger in more than two hundred plays, and whose writing seldom [rose] above a moderate level of competence" could have produced on first writing a text as free from errors and ready for production as the ms. of the quarto probably was. Speaking of Heywood's *The Captives,* he says the play "contains very little original alteration and is tidily if illegibly written, and . . . elaborately cut and annotated by the book-keeper."[25] It is quite likely that *Swetnam the Woman-hater* was printed from such a copy.[26]

Although these considerations are pertinent to the problem of authorship, they are unfortunately more interesting than conclusive. In light of the little evidence, about all one can do is agree with the hesitant suggestions of the Rev. Mr. Grosart and Professor Wright: there is circumstantial evidence that Heywood had a hand in writing *Swetnam the Woman-hater.* He was with the company at the time, and it is the kind of play he could have written and the kind of play of which he most likely would have approved.

Notes

1. Bentley, v, 1416, notes that Langbaine in his *An Account of the English Dramatick Poets* (Oxford, 1691), p. 551, identifies the source as the Juan de Flores novelette. This work was reissued in 1699, revised by C. Gildon, et al., as *The Lives and Characters of the English Dramatick Poets*, where the entry is made again on p. 169. "*Swetnam, the Woman-hater, arraign'd by Women*, a Comedy, 4to. 1620. acted at the *Red-Bull*, by the Queen's Servants. Plot from an old *Spanish* Book, call'd, *Historia de Aurelia, Isabella Hija del Rey de Escotia*, &c. 12mo. and from an *English Pamphlet*, entituled, *The Arraignment of Lewd, Idle, Froward, and Inconstant Woman*."

2. Matulka, p. xvii. Professor Matulka, as scholars before her, could not solve the problem of *Aurelio e Isabella*'s authorship. Lelio Aletiphilo is credited with the work, but that name is probably a pseudonym. It was translated from *Grisel y Mirabella* in 1521 (p. 169). Although the Rev. Mr. Grosart says in his introduction that the plot of *Swetnam* is drawn from a "Spanish work (mis)-attributed to Juan De Flores," *The History of Aurelio and Isabel* (xxxvii), and he discusses the matter at some length, he was confused about the origin of the novelette, believing that the *Aurelio e Isabella* and *Grisel Y Mirabella* were completely different works. Professor Matulka comments justifiably, it seems, that "It is, perhaps, scarcely worth while to point out the numerous errors in Grosart's introduction," and that he "fails to notice that this play follows almost scene by scene the greater part of the *Historia de Aurelio e Isabella* and that it is, in fact, the most thorough and unoriginal imitation of the novel in any play known" (219n).

3. Juan de Flores, *Grisel Y Mirabella* (i Lerida, 1495?). Sale nuevamente a luz reporducido en facsimil por acuerdo do la Real Academia Espanola (Madrid, 1954).

4. Matulka, xii.

5. The differences between *Grisel Y Mirabella* and the translated *Aurelio e Isabella* are discussed in detail by Professor Matulka.

6. Matulka, 473-475. Both of the 1556 editions were printed in Antwerp, one by Juan Latio, the other by Juan Steelsio. The 1588 edition was printed in London and licensed to Edward Aggas, Nov. 20. There were two impressions of the 1608 edition, one credited to Jean Mommart and the other to Mommart and Jean Reyne.

7. Matulka, 172.

8. Matulka, 175-176.

9. Matulka, 138.

10. III, iii, 1-3: *Enter* Atticus, Misogynos, *two Iudges, Notarie, Cryer, two Lawyers, and Attendants*—and then Lisandro, *and* Hortensia *guarded.*
III, iii, 140-141: *Hort.* Oh, but the Art/Of Woman—

11. Bentley, v, 1417.

12. F. G. Fleay, *A Biographical Chronicle of the English Drama 1599-1642,* 2 vols. (London, 1891), vol. ii, p. 332.

13. George F. Reynolds, *The Staging of Elizabethan Plays At the Red Bull Theater 1605-1625* (London, 1940), p. 21. Professor Reynolds cites Felix Schelling's *Elizabethan Drama 1558-1642,* 2 vols. (Boston and New York, 1908), which mentions the play and its source briefly in ii, 237-238.

14. E. K. Chambers, *The Elizabethan Stage,* 4 vols. (London, 1923), vol. ii, p. 448.

15. Matulka, 224.

16. Bentley, i, 164.

17. Bentley, i, 165. John T. Murray, *English Dramatic Companies 1558-1642,* 2 vols. (New York, 1910), vol. i, pp. 204-205.

18. Bentley, i, 165.

19. Bentley, v, 1417-1418. Professor Bentley cites passages from Act II, Scene 2, and III, 3.

20. Grosart, xxxiv.

21. Bentley, ii, 427-428.

22. Grosart, xlvii. He quotes from Act IV, citing Heywood's *Dramatic Works,* 1874, iii, 56, 60. The edition has been reissued by Russell & Russell, Inc. (New York, 1964) retaining the original volume numbers and pagination.

23. Wright, 490n.

24. Another consideration is one which is noted by Alfred Harbage:
> [D]espite their heroic tone these plays reveal a marked feminism. This quality was partly due to the spirit of the times, reacting against that anti-feminism of Jacobean England that had broken out in such diatribes as those by *Swetnam the Woman-hater.* However, the feminism of Cavalier drama is more directly attributable to *preciosite,* and to the fact that Cavalier plays were calculated to the meridian of court ladies, principally the Queen. Women were, after all, the most avid readers of romances.

One should remember, however, that he was concerned with a kind of drama somewhat different from and later than this 1620 play.

25. W. W. Greg, *The Editorial Problem in Shakespeare* (Oxford, 1942), p. 30.

26. Greg in his *Bibliography of the English Printed Drama,* 4 vols. (Oxford, 1939-1959), vol. ii, p .510, entry 362, says that the quarto's ornaments make it appear that the printer was William Stansby. If Stansby did print the quarto, then the argument for Heywood's authorship is somewhat weakened. A check using Paul G. Morrison's *Index of Printers, Publishers and Booksellers* (Charlottesville, 1950) does not indicate that Stansby printed any of Heywood's plays.

Chapter 3.

The Play as Literature and Theater

A typical Jacobean tragi-comedy, *Swetnam the Woman-hater* shares all of the traits usually attributed to that type of drama. It was also designed to please the "commoner" audience which frequented the Red Bull Theater, this aim fulfilled in great part by the Swetnam (Misogenos) scenes. The result of this combination of traits and aims is not the disunity that one might expect. The interweaving of the romantic, near "heroic" plot adopted from Juan de Flores and the earthy, sometimes slapstick humor based on Swetnam's antics is extremely deft. The tone of neither intrudes on the other. Where the two plots merge, at the debate to decide who is first cause of sin, man or woman, the comic aspect of the Misogenos character is adjusted just enough to make the woman-hater seem a legitimate threat to the female cause. And yet, it is not adjusted so much that it seems inconsistent with the character established in the earlier scenes. While Misogenos, in a sense, appears more respectable in this scene, Lorenzo's character and the general cause of justice loses some of its stature. This adjustment is not forced. Swetnam, in character, pursues his cause with the persistence one would expect from a fanatic. His success in the debate is the result of his singlemindedness, the same characteristic that makes him seem so ludicrous in other scenes. Lorenzo, on the other hand, to whose nobility of character and cause we are introduced earlier in the play, is less effective for the equally human reasons of temper and frustration. With Misogenos inspired by his megalomania and Lorenzo hampered by his indignation, added to the male judges' natural inclination to side with the men, the outcome of the debate is perfectly acceptable. What under other circumstances could seem absurd, the victory of the foolish and ignoble over the wise and noble, seems very understandable. And, after this scene, which apparently determines the fates of the lovers, Lisandro and Leonida, and directs the plot toward tragedy, Misogenos is returned easily to his comic status in which he again can be ridiculed.

The merging of these two plots is further facilitated by the early association of Scanfardo, who is introduced first as Nicanor's servant and partner in the plot against the crown, with Misogenos' fencing school. At the end of Act I, Scene i, we see Nicanor and Scanfardo together; the scene has been by no means a happy one. The princes, we are told, are dead, and the princess is to be locked up and guarded by the lord Nicanor, who we learn, is not favored by the princess: Nicanor tells Scanfardo,

> Oft haue I courted, bin reiected too;
> Yet what of that? I'le trye her once agen.
> What many Princes haue attempting fail'd,
> I by accesse may purchase, that's my hope;
> The King I'me sure affects mee; nothing then
> Is wanting but her loue; that once obtain'd
> Sicill is ours. *Scanfardoe!* if we win,
> Thou shalt be Lord *Nicanor,* I the King. (192-199)

In the very next scene, Misogenos and Swash are introduced, and Scanfardo again appears, this time to enter fencing school. We also learn that he is to be married; in Act II, Scene ii, Scanfardo is again on stage, and we learn that his sweetheart is Loretta, the servant-confidante of Leonida. Thus, when Loretta unwittingly betrays her mistress, it is through the character who is so far our one connection between the serious and comic episodes of the play.

We should note also that, although the Swetnam episodes were undoubtedly very popular with the Red Bull audience, as the title of the play and the picture of the "arraignment" scene on the title page tend to indicate,[1] other elements of *Swetnam the Woman-hater* would also appeal to such an audience. It would have enjoyed the blood, pageantry, and intrigue of the Lisandro-Leonida-Lorenzo story; it is offered both a masque (V, iii) and dumb show (IV, ii); a few lines after the play opens, the king enters in a death march; there is singing and dancing; the disguises and intrigue are introduced in the first act and are major to the development of the play right up to the last lines of the last scene; Leonida's apparently dead body is shown on stage, and Lisandro attempts suicide over it. All of these characteristics would have appealed at the Red Bull, would appeal today, for that matter.

And there is reason to believe that this audience would have enjoyed as much as any other those characteristics usually associated with tragicomedy. The windings of *Swetnam the Woman-hater's* improbable plot are devious enough to amuse the average audience of any time; we have the return of the supposed dead Prince Lorenzo, the plotting of the villain Nicanor, the intrigue of both Nicanor for evil and Iago for good, the chance betrayal of Leonida and Lisandro by the princess' servant, the near deaths of Lisandro and Leonida and their rescue at the last minute, Atticus' sudden change of heart and his forgiving of the lovers, Nicanor's surprising and quite unlikely repentance, and the King's equally as unlikely and surprising forgiving of him. The disguise, an expected device of the early seventeenth century stage, is much exploited: Misogenos (I, ii) is Swetnam's assumed name; Lorenzo (I, iii) returns to the court disguised; Lisandro (II, i and ii) converses with Nicanor and gains entrance to Leonida's quarters disguised as Friar Anthonie; Lorenzo dons a second disguise—this time a favorite of Elizabethan, Jacobean, and Carolinian drama—as Atlanta, a woman, the Amazon defender of women's honor; he is disguised a third time in the masque (V, iii) as an old shepherd. And this last situation offers Lorenzo disguised as Atlanta disguised as a shepherd, and before the scene is over, the audience sees both disguises thrown off.

Besides these characteristics which generally typify tragi-comedy of the time, several others deserve notice. The action begins immediately after the Battle of Lepanto, in which Lorenzo was lost; and throughout the play, until the last moments of the final scene, a threat of civil war lurks in the background. Even before the prince and princess are sentenced, Iago tells Nicanor

> ... Marke my words, *Nicanor;* Ere the Crowne
> Impale thy Temples by Her timelesse end,
> Mine and fiue thousand liues shall all expire.   (III, i, 154-156)

The return of the lost son is typical. Throughout the play the villainous determination of Nicanor to gain the throne even if it costs the princess' life is contrasted with the virtue of Lorenzo. The true and noble love between Lisandro and Leonida, each of whom is willing to die to save the other's life, is contrasted with the love Nicanor professes, a love based on his lust for both the princess and power, with the latter the more important. It is contrasted also with the love between the servants Scanfardo and Loretta, an apparently baser love, consisting chiefly in physical desire. This love is also less important, at least to Scanfardo, than mercenary considerations. After Loretta has told him that the princess and Lisandro are alone in the princess' chamber and has invited Scanfardo to her bed, he observes that

> Venerie is sweet.
> But he that has good store of gold and wealth,
> May haue it at command, and not by stealth.   (II, ii, 161-163)

The servant and his master are apparently much alike. Finally, although there is no actual *deus ex machina,* we must recognize Lorenzo's presence and his and Iago's abilities to bring people back to life, or, at least, save them from what seems to be sure death, as being akin to such a device. The masque itself which, although no amount of pressure from other sources has convinced him, manages to bring Atticus to his senses, is also a kind of *deus ex machina.*

The play differs from many tragi-comedies in at least two ways, the first being the obvious concern of *Swetnam the Woman-hater* with matters other than noble love. That concern, of course, is seen in the Swetnam plot, the major consideration of which is not really the threat of Leonida's life, but Swetnam's "slanders" against women in general. The second difference is less substantial, and one that seems to lead naturally to a consideration of character. Although Lorenzo, the heroic figure, stands for nobility and virtue, he is by no means a perfect example of such. His loss of the debate, at least partially because of temper, and his initial overreaction to Swetnam's anti-feminism have already been touched upon. His first inclination after hearing Swetnam is to uphold the honor of women, "who's iust fame/Merits an Angels Pen to register" (III, ii, 57-58), in spite of indications that neither he, Iago, nor anyone else has such extreme views. This, in some ways minor, aspect of Lorenzo's character is consistent with his actions during the debate.

However, as we have noted before, Lorenzo, Leonida, and Lisandro are not the most interesting or the best drawn characters in the play. Perhaps the most interesting, and most fully-developed character is Loretta, Leonida's fun-loving and faithful servant and confidante. (It is the playwright's knack with the comic and earthy element of the drama that tempts one to associate him with the talents of late Elizabethan writers. Of all the characters, she more than any of the others reflects the Elizabethan spirit of fun that was so well represented about twenty years earlier.) Loretta[2] remains sympathetic and "good," if human. The only other character who approaches her in touches of earthy realism is Swash, the clown; and he, almost by definition, is responsible for too much slapstick to appear as "real" as Loretta. She is first seen in Act II, Scene i, with Lisandro, to whom she promises loyalty and help in his suit for Leonida's hand. At the close of this meeting, she takes a "gift" from the prince, concluding, "I must confesse,/*Lisandro* is a Noble Gentleman, and has good gifts" (II, i, 57-58). Next, in the same scene, she promises to help Nicanor in his suit. However, she never really lies; she tells Nicanor that Leonida does not care for him. After Nicanor instructs her to sue for him, she waits until she can get a gift from him. Thus, though she obviously favors Lisandro and dislikes Nicanor, she manages, without lying, to profit from both men. It is in the next scene with Leonida that she presses Nicanor's suit, after teasing

Leonida with the information that she has seen Lisandro; and she ends her praise of the old prince with

> Who doe you think's in loue with you?
> The old Dragon *Nicanor,* that watches the fruit of your
> *Hesperides.* (II, ii, 35-37)

She has not gone back on her word to Nicanor, but still she has not compromised herself.

Loretta is, throughout her short role, which virtually ends in Act II, a playful servant; and she is a delightful character. One of her especially appealing traits is her apparent obsession with what her betters do. Although this comment on the behavior of servants is undoubtedly meant as an incidental "moral" in the play, it is mostly fun when Loretta observes, after taking the gift from Lisandro, "that, wee poore Gentlewomen, that haue no other fortunes but our attendance, must now and then make the best vse of our places: wee haue president, and very lately too" (II, i, 59-64). And, later, after she has hurried Lisandro and Leonida into another chamber to be alone for what she happily assumes to be illicit love making, she wishes that Scanfardo were with her, for

> ... if he were here now, I would
> Neuer cast such an vnwilling deniall vpon him
> As I haue done, hauing so good a president as I haue. (II, ii, 107-109)

She would have them, as Scanfardo says,

> ... eu'n doe,
> As our betters haue done before vs,
> The example is easly followed,
> Hauing so good a Schoole-mistris.
> Shall we to bed? (II, ii, 138-142)

But, even so, Loretta will not deny herself the privilege of answering,

> Fye, seruant, how you talke?
> Troth you are to blame, to offer to assault
> The chastitie of any Gentlewoman,
> Vpon aduantage. (II, ii, 142-145)

We have here both the pleasure of an insight into the character of Loretta and a comment on the central question of the play and the later debate between the men and the women.

Among the other interesting characters are Atticus and Aurelia, although Aurelia has very few scenes. Atticus moves from an object of pity in the first scene because of factors beyond his control, the deaths of his sons, to an object of pity in the later scenes because of his weakness, an inability to temper justice with mercy and the failure to recognize the authority of noble love. Furthermore, the death sentence of Leonida and the exile of Lisandro seem not only unreasonable and cruel but unjust because there is always some doubt as to whether the couple were guilty of anything more than being in one another's company: Lisandro swears to the innocence of the meeting, and at the play's end even the suspicious king is willing to accept this story. Atticus' obsession with "justice" and being marked by posterity as the just king is central to his character and the development of the plot. That he always has been deeply concerned with the question of justice is reflected in Iago's speech to the disguised Lorenzo. As one of the king's close counselors, probably he is likely to describe the king in terms of what is the court's major concern.

> Men call him, Sir, The iust King Atticus;
> And truly too: for with an equall Scale
> He waighes the offences betwixt man and man;
> He is not sooth'd with adulation,
> Nor mou'd with teares, to wrest the course of Iustice
> Into an vniust current, to oppresse
> The Innocent; nor do's he make the Lawes
> Punish the man, but in the man the cause. (I, iii, 5-12)
>
> . . . .
>
> His state is full of maiestie and grace,
> Whose basis is true Pietie and Vertue,
> Where, vnderneath a rich triumphant Arch,
> That does resemble the Tribunall Seat,
> Garded with Angels, borne vpon two Columnes,
> Iustice and Clemencie, he sits inthron'd.
> His subiects serue him freely, not perforce,
> And doe obey him more for loue, then feare;
> Being a King not of themselues alone,
> And their estates, but their affections:
> A soueraigntie that farre more safetie brings,
> Then do's an Armie to the guard of Kings. (15-26)

These lines prepare us well for what Atticus is to do and say later, and they contain much irony. His scale weighs equally "the offences betwixt man and man." How about between man and woman? He is not "mou'd with teares"; he refuses to be moved by pleas for Leonida. But then he is sued not "to wrest the course of Iustice/ Into an vniust current," but to save the innocent. In his quest for justice, he will "make the Lawes/ Punish the man." The second angel, "Clemencie," will be forgotten. His subjects' opinion of him will change radically after the sentencing of Leonida and Lisandro: they will obey more from fear than love. Sforza will warn Iago to "Forbeare, my Lord, the times are dangerous" (IV, i, 34), and later the guards who allow Lisandro the chance to kill himself will choose to fight in the foreign war rather than stay in the country to face the king. When asked what action seems best, the first guard exclaims

> There is no way but one, let's leaue the Land:
> If we stay heere, we shall be sure to dye,
> And suffer for our too much lenitie,
> Though we are innocent. (IV, v, 54-57)

And, of course, the loss of the quality, that Iago says protects Atticus better than an army could, will result in the danger of civil war.

Atticus' "fall" is ascribable to several causes. His disappointment with Leonida may be considered the last of a series of heavy personal blows: the loss of his two sons (added to the usual burdens of kingship), and finally Leonida's apparent crime are just too much for him. One must also consider the deep loss of faith and pride he suffers when his own daughter disobeys a royal command.

> How full of troubles is the state of Kings,
> Abroad, with Foes, at home, with faithlesse Friends,
> Within with cares, without, a thousand feares!
> Yet all summ'd vp together, doth not make
> Such an impression in our troubled thoughts,
> As this one Act of disobedience
> In our owne Issue. (III, i, 3-9)

A further reason is the frustration Atticus previously has suffered with his daughter; her final act of defiance leads him to exasperation. Leonida, we learn early, has been a great deal of trouble. In Act I, Scene i, we learn how the king feels.

> The Girle is wanton, coy, and fickle too:
> How many Princes hath the froward Elfe
> Set at debate, desiring but her loue?
> What dangers may insue? (I, i, 162-165)

To aggravate matters further her latest suitor, Lisandro, is far from being one of the king's favorites.

> Shee shall not wed with that presumptuous Boy,
> His father and Our selfe were still at oddes, (I, i, 172-173)

Iago later explains that her fame has attracted

> The chiefe Italian Princes, but their Loues
> Were quitted with contempt and crueltie:
> And many of our braue Sicilian Youths
> Haue sacrific'd their liues to her disdaine.
> Now to preuent the like euent hereafter,
> 'Twas thought fit her libertie should be awhile restraind, (I, iii, 47-52)

There are even those who apparently believe the death sentence may be justified. Iago pleads with Sforza to join in an appeal for Leonida's life.

> Oh 'tis a royall Princesse, faire, and chaste!
>   *Sforz.* But her disdaine, my Lord, hath bin the cause
> Of many hopefull Youths vntimely end;
> 'Tis that has harden'd both the Commons hearts,
> And many a noble Peeres.
>   *Iago.*   Why, what of that?
> It is not fit affection should be forc'd:
> Let's kneele vnto his Grace for her release.
> Iustice (like Lightning) euer should appear
> To few mens ruine, but to all mens feare.   (IV, i, 81-90)

Indeed, one may be as much amazed at Iago's attitude, saner though it may be, as at Sforza's.

Iago's last two lines, which J. P. Collier praises highly,[3] are of major importance because they express the sentiment (undoubtedly approved by the playwright), which Atticus forgets in his presumption. Excessive pride in his reputation as a just king, excessive faith in his ability to determine what is and is not just, and excessive desire to be noted by history as the most just of rulers are the important reasons for Atticus' decline as a person and as a king. Before any action is taken in Lisandro and Leonida's case, Atticus reveals himself to the audience. At the very beginning of Act III, Scene i, immediately following the Act II discovery of the prince and princess together, he makes clear which it is he loves more, his children or fame with posterity.

> Bring to the Barre the Prisoners: this offence
> Hath lost in vs a Father and a Friend,
> And cals for Iustice from vs, as a King:
> Yet thinke not, Lords, but 'tis with griefe of mind,
> Nor can a Father easly forget
> A Daughter whom hee once so dearely lou'd:
> Yet we had rather become Issulesse,
> Then leaue it noted to Posteritie,
> An Act of such Iniustice.   (13-21)

The irony in the closely following statement, contained in his instruction to the judges, is very interesting in light of the plot's development and the man-woman question.

> Therefore, my Lords, you that sit here to Iudge,
> Let all respect of persons be forgot,
> And deale vprightly, that you may resemble
> The highest Iudge, whose seat on Earth you hold:
> And for you know, the Lawes of Sicilie
> Forbid to punish two, for one offence,

> Let your care be to find the principall,
> The *Primus Motor* that begun the cause;
> For the effect (you see) is but the issue
> That one of them may worthily receiue
> Deserued death; the other, may be sent
> (As lesse offending) into banishment. (32-43)

Atticus calls on them to "resemble/ The highest Iudge," but in the very next line invokes "the Lawes of Sicilie." These earth-made laws assume that the kind of sin of which Lisandro and Leonida are presumably guilty is the fault of one party or the other, although the question has never been settled, either by theologians or politicians; and the possibility that both men and women are equally guilty (or responsible) is never mentioned by either Atticus or the judges. Is is certainly presumptuous to assume that one should "worthily receiue/ Deserued death" and that the other is "lesse offending." It is reasonable to suppose that both the theater and reading audiences would be aware of the problem posed by Atticus' and the law's attitude; neither the play nor, of course, the controversy would have existed if the premise of this fictional law were not generally in question. It is the general doubt about this question in the audience's mind and the apparent surety in the king's mind that comprises the significant ironic element. Atticus' assumption that the law is sound—or rather his failure to question the law under conditions which ought especially to provoke such questioning—is instrumental in his downfall and the progress of the action. The very shallowness of Atticus' conception of justice in this the only case with which the audience can be familiar is a characteristic compatible with his megalomaniac concern with how posterity will judge him. His faith in the abstraction, Justice, leads him to another ironic statement. Although Justice has become almost an idol to him, he cannot see even her concrete representation accurately.

> It is impossible
> That sacred Iustice should be hudwink't still,
> Though she be falsly painted so; Her eyes
> Are cleare, and so perspicuous, that no cryme
> Can maske it selfe in any borrowed shape,
> But shee'le discouer it. Let vm be returnd
> Back to their seuerall Wards, till we deuise
> Some better course for the discouery. (III, i, 130-137)

Atticus (seeing what he really believes is himself in the role of Justice) assumes only that there must be another method that will find the truth, truth which he has determined partially already. Removing the blindfold which prohibits the distortion of emotional consideration, he humanizes his goddess and negates the immortal virtue for which she was deified. He here, as well as at the debate, refuses to accept evidence in favor of mutual guilt. But his pride in reputation cannot allow him reason now. After the sentences have been carried out, Atticus asks for a report.

> How took the Girle her death? did she not raue?
> Exclaime vpon me for the Iustice done
> By a iust Father? (V, i, 2-4)

He ironically asks those around him why they stand "Like so many sencelesse Statues," as if there were "an eclipse,/ Betwixt your iudgements and affections" (8-10). He would have acted differently, he reveals,

> But, that the World should know our equitie,
> Were she a thousand daughters she should die. (23-24)

Atticus, although not a great dramatic character, is an interesting one.

None of the other characters has so much written for him. Lorenzo, discussed previously, offers chances to an actor who might wish to make the most of his tendency to impulsiveness. Aurelia appears very seldom, but often enough to be an effective nagging wife. The contrast, in almost every scene they share, between the dignity Atticus in part affects, and the emotionality Aurelia explodes with, offers stage possibilities. Lisandro is little more than the stock noble lover, willing to sacrifice all for his sweetheart. His suicide speech, however, is not without some merit. Leonida is never as interesting as the descriptions of her promise. Although Nicanor has three thematic dimensions—the villain ambitious for the throne at any cost, the old and unwelcome suitor in the January-May conflict, and the "evil" counselor, in contrast with Iago, the "good" counselor (recalling the traditional good angel-bad angel combat)—he is not very interesting as a human being or even as the statement of the universal problem. Iago is the spokesman for good sense, the loyal subject, and wise counselor; he offers that and little more to the audience, although there are possibilities, perhaps, of the same kind one sees in Lorenzo. He seems abrupt with those with whom he disagrees; he is quick to challenge Nicanor (some natural jealousy, of course, exists between them); and there is his peculiar absence from the debate scene, a fact which provides the playwright a chance to review the action for the audience and establish what the writer undoubtedly believes should be the proper response to Misogenos and the outcome of the trial.

Swash can be considered more properly a successful convention than a character. The usual fool who is not so foolish, Swash entertains with both slapstick and word play, and, although he is Swetnam's constant companion and servant, he is willing throughout for the punishment of his master. Among other well-executed conventions is the use of the letter, especially that from Leonida to Lisandro (II, i). Present also are the conventional comments on current problems. Loretta's concern with the example set by her superiors is in the same courtesy-book tradition as the play's lessons in kingship. There are some typical comments on the clergy. The very fact that Friar Anthony allows Lisandro his frock to help the prince disobey the king's command and visit the princess' chamber is comment in itself. Nicanor voices an uncomplimentary attitude when he considers appealing for his help.

> I could not thinke vpon a better Agent.
> Their seeming sanctitie makes all their acts
> Sauour of Truth, Religion, Pietie,   (II, i, 130-132)

The Rev. Mr. Grosart notes a comment on the lives of the soldiers in the scene in which the Captain reports to Atticus on the fate of Lorenzo.[4] Atticus offers him a reward, and he accepts.

> I'le not be nice in the refusall, Sir,
> It is no wonder t'see a Souldier want: (I, i, 151-152)

Perhaps something more may be said here about the general stageability of *Swetnam the Woman-hater*. Much has been made of the "arraignment" scene in which Swetnam, Swash, and the women clown both physically and verbally. There are other aspects of the play that contribute to its being good theater. The quick movement of the entire play—even the fourth act which contains the conventional dumb show and song—helps it much. There are such little touches as scene iv of this act, between the two gentlemen who discuss the king's decree.[5] Although the scene is only 10 lines long, it heightens the drama by making it seem momentarily that the decision is irrevocable and that the princess is already dead. However, what makes the play most obviously the work of a man familiar with the theater is not the evidence of one act or scene, but the stageability of each and the contribution of each right up to the play's resolution—the saving of Lisandro and Leonida and the last mintue repentance of Atticus and reform of Nicanor.

The playwright's theatrical skill is evidenced by factors which range from the humor of such exchanges as the following,

> *Loren.* Is't possible! that Sicilie should breed
> Such a degenerate Monster, shame of men?
> *Iago.* Blame not your Countrie, he's an Englishman.   (III, ii, 48-50)

to the manner with which the author handles the device of the letter. A letter from Misogenos to Atlanta is later delivered to Atlanta by Swash. After Swash hands the letter to her (Lorenzo in disguise), he is engaged by Aurelia; opportunity is provided for some clowning, and at the same time Lorenzo is given time to read the letter. When Lorenzo finishes the letter and gives it to Aurelia to read aloud, the prince is free to react to what he hears, verbally after every few lines, not as one to whom the letter has been newly revealed, but as a person who at the moment, is planning on information already received. Such a structure, more interesting than one based on mutual, synchronic revelation, allows for more vocal and pictorial variety on stage, something which may or may not be desirable, depending on the judgment of those staging the play. One can point also to the effectiveness of Aurelia's "mad" scene (V, i), Iago's description of how Leonida faced her "death" (V, i), or Loretta's exchange with Leonida during her "suit" for Nicanor.

There are, expectedly, weaknesses in *Swetnam the Woman-hater,* many of which stem from the tragi-comic form itself, a disappointing one to many. The abruptness of the ending should not be of much concern, even if the turn of events is less smoothly executed than it might be. The playwright's audience, familiar with the form, and aware that Swetnam's role was being taken too lightly for the play to be tragic, doubtlessly expected such an ending; and the author certainly had prepared them, at least for the saving of Leonida and Lisandro. When Atticus grants Lorenzo's request that Leonida

>   not basely
> Be hurried forth amongst vnciuill men;
> But that your Queene, and I, and some few others,
> With any one of your attendant Lords,
> May see her execution.   (III, iii, 284-288)

the conditions under which she may be saved are set. Later, when Lorenzo soliloquizes over Leonida's body, he says,

> Me thinkes, I feele fresh heat, as if her soule
> Had resum'd her former seate agen,   (IV, v, 44-45)

and fewer than 20 lines after he stabs himself, the audience is told that he is not dead. Lorenzo comes upon his body.

>   See, he looks vp,
> Ile beare him out of the ayre, and stop his wound:
> If there be any hope, I haue a Balme
> Of knowne experience, in effecting cures
> Almost impossible, and if the wound
> Be not too deadly, will recouer him.   (68-73)

There are many more important weaknesses other than the abruptness of the resolution. The shallowness of characterization, especially of

Lorenzo, Lisandro, and Leonida, is apparent. That following Act II both Loretta and Scanfardo disappear from the action is disappointing. There are apparent inconsistencies. Although Atticus first says that he and the king of Naples (Lisandro's father) are not on good terms and that Lisandro is a "presumptuous Boy" (I, i, 172), he later refers to the prince as a friend (III, i, 14). The apparent conflict between the houses of Naples and Sicily is never exploited. One wonders, also, how a prince can be exiled from a country of which he is not a native. Such a punishment does not seem very effective. All in all, however, *Swetnam the Woman-hater* is a pretty good example of Jacobean tragicomedy, and it is a much better play than the long lack of modern edition would suggest.

Notes

1. See chapter one concerning the remarks of Professors Bentley and Reynolds.

2. The importance of Loretta's character to the feminist question in the play is discussed in chapter one. Some of this discussion is pertinent to Loretta's success as a character for other than thematic considerations.

3. J. P. Collier, *The History of English Dramatic Poetry,* 3 vols. (London, 1831), vol. iii, p. 325-326n. Professor Collier says the play "contains some fine writing, and is a highly creditable performance." He cites the couplet in question and says that it "is one of the noblest and justest images in our language. . . . far better than Webster's celebrated simile, which is neither noble nor just." The Webster couplet he refers to is the following found in *The Duchess of Malfi* (Act I, Scene i) and first used in *The White Devil.*

> Glories, like glow-worms afar off shine bright,
> But look'd to near, have neither heat nor light.

the Rev. Mr. Grosart (xliv) cites Professor Collier, and he himself praises the play (xlii-xliii) as having "lines and phrases declarative of restrained power alike of imagination and expression."

4. See the Rev. Mr. Grosart's comment in the Glossarial and Explanatory Notes.

5. A discussion of the problems presented by this scene may be found in the Textual Notes.

Swetnam the Woman-hater,
Arraigned by Women

A Note on the Text

The copy text for the present edition is the only quarto extant, the 1620 edition printed for Richard Meighen.[1] Only two press variants occur in the ten copies collated.[2] I have collated also Alexander Grosart's edition, the only known reprint, adopting changes suggested by him where they seemed to accord with modern editing standards. Occasional use also has been made of the J. S. Farmer's facsimile (1914), which reproduced the Dyce copy.[3]

I have adopted moderate editorial principles. Although I have accepted almost all of the substantive readings of the quarto, I have corrected all errors which are clearly of compositorial origin. These, happily, are few in number. My policy in the emendation of accidentals is conservative: I have left virtually unaltered the spelling of the quarto; I have emended capitalization in only those few places where changes in lineation seemed proper; and I have altered punctuation only when I found that of the quarto clearly misleading. Often, where Grosart felt a semi-colon should be substituted for a comma, or a comma should be placed before "and" to punctuate elements in a series, I have allowed the quarto's punctuation to stand. All emendations are recorded at the bottom of the page on which they occur. Where an emendation, particularly one that is substantive or semi-substantive, calls for comment, I have treated it in a textual note at the end of the edition.

Changes in lineation are noted wherever they occur because of the great difficulty one experiences in differentiating verse from poetic prose. I detect but few compositorial errors in the verse lineation, but where I have emended, I have usually discussed the problem in a textual note. In a few ambiguous instances where choice seemed arbitrary, I have let the quarto arrangement stand. In deciding whether a speech is poetry or prose, I have considered not only scansion but also the character in question, the context, and the mood of the scene.

In general, stage directions follow the arrangement in the quarto; entrances are centered; *Aside* and other such interpolations which fall within the text of a speech appear in square brackets before the first word of the speech involved; all other directions appear in the right

A Note on the Text 49

hand margin. I have silently expanded such abbreviations as *Ex.* and *Scen.,* but I have noted any change from *Exit* to *Exeunt* or *vice versa.*

I have normalized speech headings, usually using the first five letters of the character's name, e.g., *Nican* for *Nicanor, Attic* for *Atticus, Loret* for *Loretta,* etc. For *Leonida* and *Gentleman* I have used the abbreviations *Leon* and *Gent,* on the assumption that a concluding consonant is preferable to a vowel. Those speech headings which appear infrequently (e.g. *Old Woman, Young Woman, Lawyer, Notarie,* and *Herald*) are spelled out. In all but the last three speech headings in V, iii, the quarto substitutes *King* for *Atticus;* I have normalized these to *Attic.* The names *Scanfardoe* and *Misogynos* are also spelled *Scanfardo and Misogenos,* and these variations are retained. In the very few instances in which emendations of the speech headings involve substantives, I footnote each change and discuss it in the textual notes.

I have silently expanded ampersands, tildes, and other similar abbreviations, and normalized wrong fonts and factota. Roman numerals used in the quarto to designate scenes have been silently changed from capital to lower case, e.g., III to iii. Scene divisions which I have added are in square brackets. They are not usually discussed because the reason for the division is usually an obvious shift of location. I have silently put flush left all speeches which are cramped on one line in the quarto to save the printer space. Such variations in spelling as *I'le and Ile, I'me* and *Ime,* and other inconsistent uses of the apostrophe are left as they appear in the quarto. The long "s" has been modernized, but the use of "u," "v," "i," and "j" has been retained. The quarto's use of italic and Roman type has also been retained. I have, however, changed italic proper names to Roman in some places, and these changes are recorded.

The footnotes deal with all emendations, not just substantive and semi-substantive matters. In every case the lemma is from the present text, and the reading of the quarto follows the square bracket. If Grosart's reading has been followed, the siglum, G, followed by a semicolon, appears between the square bracket and the quarto reading.

Following the text are a Table of Grosart's Emendations, Textual Notes, and Glossarial and Explanatory notes. The Table of Grosart's Emendations includes all those changes suggested by Grosart in either his text or the notes following his text, notes which often suggest changes of mind; Grosart's edition was printed before the notes, and apparently it was impossible for him to change the text itself. Changes suggested in his notes, which very properly may be called "afterthoughts," are designated by the symbol, G2. The Textual Notes discuss some of the emendations and refusals to emend indicated in the footnotes. Such allusions and vocabulary which might not be readily recognized by a reader of Elizabethan or Jacobean drama are discussed in the Glossarial and Explanatory Notes.

The question of compositor determination is a difficult one. Results of the usual spelling and typographical tests are inconclusive. Variant spelling seems indiscriminate. For instance, on B signature, although the spelling *Ile* occurs five times, the spelling *I'll* occurs also. *Ime* occurs once, as does *I'm*. Other spelling tests also seem as inconclusive. The only two names with significant variant spellings are *Misogynos* (which also occurs *Misogenos*) and *Scanfardo* (which also occurs *Scanfardoe*). The names occur together on the same page four times: first in the "Actorvm Nomina" on the titlepage verso with the *-ynos* and *-do* endings; second on A4^V with *-enos* and *-do;* next on E with *-ynos* and *-do;* and last on F4^V with *-ynos* and *-doe*. The *-enos* ending occurs only twice in the entire quarto, once on A4^V and earlier on A4 with the word *Misogenysts*. There was very likely one compositor, or two of similar competence and inclination who worked closely together. The spelling variants might be mainly those of the ms. from which the quarto was set, and I have discussed this aspect in chapter two, section III. Greg, in a note to his bibliographical description,[4] says that the ornaments used show that the printer was probably William Stansby.[5] The Greg entry number is 362.

There remains something to be said of Grosart's edition, the only reprint of the play. His is, as all are, conservative in some matters and rather liberal in others. However, it seems that for the most part, he was conservative where he might, according to modern practice, have exercised more freedom and free where he could have stayed to the text of the quarto. He is also inconsistent in many matters. For example, his policy, on one hand, was to retain as much of the quarto as possible, including the pagination, signatures, and catch words. He retains the long "s" which I have modernized. He even carefully retains the press variants, or what should have seemed obvious typographical errors, and he preserves the quarto's erroneous references to Hortensia, although, of course, no such character occurs in the play. He normalizes neither the speech headings nor stage directions. On the other hand, he changes lineation where he feels such emendation is called for, and he freely adds words, shows contractions of the pronoun and copula or "have," and marks elisions where he feels the meter requires these changes. For instance, he often writes *I am* as *I'm; you are* as *you're;* and *I have* as *I've*. He marks such elisions as *th'offences* for *the offences* (I, iii, 7) and *t'obserue* for *to obserue* (I, iii, 3). He adds an apostrophe to show the possessive, but he is very inconsistent, adding it in some places and forgetting it in others. It should be noted, however, that in his introductory section, marked "re-readings," he says of his contractions and elisions:

> But of course the words can be read in the time of our half-foot without being written in a contracted form. Compare *Henry V:* 'We are glad the Daughter is so pleasant with us.' Mr. Ruskin, in a recent Magazine Article, is violent against one editor for writing 'We're.' (xlvi)

And of his change from *Euen* to *E'un,* he says that "perhaps it is better to print *Euen* at length, though scanning it as a monosyllable" (xlvi). Another of Grosart's practices which I have not followed is his replacement of the comma with the semi-colon, his practice being excessive by our standards. After all is said and done, however, one must recognize Grosart's work, and many of his suggestions, as extremely helpful.

The title page of the quarto is as follows:

> SWETNAM,/THE VVoman-hater,/ARRAIGNED BY WOMEN./*A new Comedie,* Acted at the *Red Bull,* by the late/Queenes Seruants./ [A woodcut, 4″ x 3 1/10″, showing a man standing at the bar before a queen. All the spectators and officials are women. The name *Swetnam* is printed vertically next to the male figure.]/LONDON,/Printed for *Richard Meighen,* and are to be ſold at his Shops/at Saint *Clements* Church, ouer-againſt *Eſſex* Houſe, and/ at *Weſtminster* Hall. 1620.

Notes

1. The copies used are referred to by the following abbreviations: CSmH, Huntington; Cty, Yale; Dfo, Folger; ICU, University of Chicago; IU, University of Illinois; MB, Boston Public Library; MH, Harvard; C, Chapin; NNP, Pierpont Morgan; and TxU, University of Texas.

2. These Press variants occur on sig. A2 recto, Act I, Scene i, lines 84 and 89 as follows:

>   84 *Nicanor.*] *Nicano.*
>   89 *Leonida,*] *Leomida,*

Uncorrected copies are NNP, MH, TxU, and CSmH.

3. *Swetnam the Woman-hater,* ed. John S. Farmer, The Tudor Facsimile Texts (London, 1914).

4. W. W. Greg, *Bibliography of the English Printed Drama,* 4 vols. (Ox- 1939-1959), vol. ii, p. 510.

5. For a statement of the consequences of William Stansby's projected printing of the quarto on the question of authorship, see chapter two, section III.

Actorvm Nomina.

Atticus, *King of Sicilie.*
Lorenzo, *his Sonne.*
Lisandro, *Prince of Naples.*
Iago,
Sforza,   } *three Noblemen*
Nicanor, } *of Sicilie.*
Scanfardo, *Seruant to* Nicanor.
Two Gentlemen.
A Captaine.
Swetnam, *alias,* Misogynos, *The Woman-hater.*   10
Swash, *his Man.*
Two Iudges.
Notarie.
Cryer.
Two Lawyers.
Three or foure Guards.

Womens Parts

Aurelia, *Queene.*
Leonida, *the Princesse.*
Loretta, *her Maid.*
Three or foure other Women.   20

---

15 Actorvm Nomina   *Two Lawyers.*] om.
16 Actorvm Nomina   *Three or foure Guards.*] om.

Enter Loretta,

Prologvs.

The Women are all welcome; for the men,
They will be welcome: our care's not for them.
'Tis we, poore women, that must stand the brunt
Of this dayes tryall: we are all accused.
How wee shall cleere our selues, there lyes the doubt.
The men, I know, will laugh, when they shall heare
Vs rayl'd at, and abused; and say, 'Tis well,
We all deserue as much. Let um laugh on,   10
Lend but your kind assistance; you shall see
We will not be ore-come with Infamie,
And slanders that we neuer merited.
Be but you patient, I dare boldly say,
(If euer women pleased) weele please to day.
    Vouchsafe to reade, I dare presume to say,
    Yee shall be pleased; and thinke 'tis a good play.

Act I. Scene. i.

Enter Iago *and* Nicanor, *two Noblemen of* Sicilia, *in priuate conference.*

Nican. Hee was a vertuous and a hopefull Prince,
And we haue iust cause to lament his death,
For had he liu'd, and Spaine made war agen,
He would ha' prou'd a Terror to his Foe.
 Iago. A greater cause of griefe was neuer knowne,
Not onely in his death, but for the losse
Of Prince *Lorenzo* too, his yonger brother,   10
Who hath beene missing almost eighteene moneths,
And none can tell whether aliue or dead.
 Nican. How do's the King beare these afflictions?

Enter another Lord.

 Iago. Now you shall heare how fares his Maiestie.
 Lord. Oh my good Lords, our sorrowes still increase,
A greater tide of woe is to be fear'd,
The Kings decay, with griefe for his two sonnes.
 Iago. The gods forbid, let's in and comfort him.
 3. *Lord.* Alas, his sorrow's such   20
He will not suffer vs to speake to him,
But turnes away in rage, and seemes to tread
The pace of one (if liuing) liuing dead.
 Iago. See where he comes, Lords, let vs all attend,
Vntill his grace he pleas'd to speake to vs.

Enter King *in black, reading.*
Dead March.

 Attic. "Death is the ease of paine, and end of sorrow."
How can that be? Death gaue my sorrowes life,
For by his death my paine and griefe begun,   30
And in beginning, neuer will haue end: for though I die,

---
24 comes, Lords,] comes, / Lords,
26 SD *Enter* .. , *reading*] flush right, lined with the second half of line 24 in Q
28 "Death . . . sorrow."] Death . . . sorrow,

55

My losse will liue in future memorie,
I, and (perhaps) will be lamented too,
And registered by some, when all shall heare
Sicilia had two sonnes, yet had no heire.
Ha! What are you?
Who dares presume to interrupt vs thus?
What meanes this sorrow? Wherefore are these signes?
Or vnto whom are these obseruances?
   Nican. Vnto our King.
   3. *Lord.*   To you my Soueraigne.   40
   Iago. Your Subiects all lament to see you sad.
   Attic. You all are Traytors then, and by my life
I will account you so:
Can you not be content with State and rule,
But you must come to take away my Crowne?
For solitude is sorrowes chiefest Crowne.
Griefe hath resign'd ouer his right to mee,
And I am King of all woes Monarchie.
You powers that grant Regeneration,
What meant you first to giue him vitall breath?   50
And make large Kingdomes proud of such a Prince
As my *Lusyppus* was, so good, so vertuous:
Then, in his prime of yeares,
To take him from mee by vntimely death?
Oh! had my spirit wings, I would ascend
And fetch his soule againe from—
Oh my sad sorrowes! Whither am I driuen?
Into what maze of errors will you lead mee?
This Monster (Griefe) hath so distracted mee,
I had almost forgot mortalitie.   60
   Iago. Deare Lord haue patience; though the heauens are pleas'd
To punish Princes for their Subiects faults,
In taking from vs such a hopefull Prince,
No doubt they will restore your yonger sonne,
Who cannot be but stay'd, and will, I hope

---

   33 I,] ~ ‸
   40 3. *Lord.*] 3. *Lords.*
   61 patience;] G2; ~,

Be quickly heard of, to recall your ioyes.
 Attic. No, I shall neuer see *Lorenzo* more,
This eighteene moneths I haue not heard of him;
I feare some Traytors hand had seyz'd his life:
If hee were liuing, as that cannot bee;   70
I sooner looke to see me dead then hee:
For I am almost spent; This heape of age,
Mixt with my sorrow, soone will end my dayes.
 Nican. My Liege, take comfort, I (your Subiect) vow
To goe my selfe to seeke *Lorenzo* forth,
And ne'r returne vntill I find him out,
Or bring some newes what is become of him.
 3. Lord. The like will I, or ne'r come backe agen.
 Iago. Old as I am, I'le not be last behind,
And if my Soueraigne please to let mee goe.   80
 Attic. I thanke your loues, but I'le restrain your wils:
If I should part from you, my dayes were done,
For I should neuer liue till your returne.
Nicanor my deare friend, *Iago, Sforza,*
One of you three, if I die issuelesse,
Must after mee be King of Sicilie.
Doe not forsake mee then.
 Omnes.   Long liue your grace:
And may your issue raigne eternally.
 Attic. As for our daughter fayre *Leonida,*
Her female Sexe cannot inherit here,   90
One must inioy both her and Sicilie.   *Shout within.*
What sudden shout was that? Some know the cause;
Can there be so much ioy left in our Land,
To raise mens voyces to so high a sound?

     Exit Nicanor, *then Re-enter.*

Or wast a shreeke of some new miserie?
For comfort cannot be expected here.
The newes, *Nicanor.*   *Trumpets.*

---

  68 him;] G; ~,
  71 me] the
  83 returne.] ~,
  83/84 SD∧] *Enter Nicanor.*
  95 *Exit* Nicanor, *then Re-enter.*] *Enter Nicanor.*

Nican.   Happie, Sir, I hope,
There is a Souldier new arriu'd at Court,
Can tell some tidings of the long lost Prince.   100
  Sforz. Sir, shall he haue accesse?
  Iago.   Oh ioyfull newes!
  Attic. Is it a question, *Sforza?* Bring him in,
As you would doe some great Ambassadour;   *Exit* Sforza.
He is no lesse. Comes he not from a Prince?
He do's, if from *Lorenzo* hee be sent.

    A flourish, with Trumpets. Enter a Captaine,
  brought in by the Lord Sforza *followed by* Scanfardoe.

Thou Man of Warre, once play the Orator,
Proue Griefe a guiltie Thiefe, condemne my feares,
And let my sorrowes suffer in these teares: 110
Haue I a sonne or no? Good Souldier speake.
  Capt. Sir, I arriu'd by chance vpon your coast,
Yet hearing of the Proclamation
Which promis'd thousands vnto any man
That could bring newes to the Sicilian King,
Whether *Lorenzo* were aliue or dead—
  Attic. We'le double our reward what-e'r it be,
If hee be liuing: Dead, we'le keepe our word:
Then prethee say, What is become of him?
  Capt. Not for reward, but loue to that braue Prince,   120
Whose memorie deserues to out-liue time,
Come I to tell what I too truely know;
In the Lepanthean battel not long since,
Where he was made Commander of a Fleet,
Vnder Don *Iohn* the Spanish Generall,
He did demeane himselfe so manfully,
That he perform'd wonders aboue beliefe;
For when the Nauies ioyn'd, the Cannons plaid,
And thundring clamors rang the dying knels
Of many thousand soules; He, void of feare,   130

---
   100 Prince.] ~:
   103 SD *Exit* Sforza.] om.
   107 SD Sforza *followed by*] om.   Scanfardoe.] *Scanfardoe.*
   116 dead—] ~.
   128 the Nauies] the the Nauies

Dalli'd with danger, and pursu'd the Foe
Thorow a bloudy Sea of Victorie:
Whether there slaine, or taken prisoner
By the too mercilesse misbeleeuing Turkes,
No man can tell:
That when Victorie fell to the Christians,
The conquest, and the glorie of the day
Was soone eclipst, in braue *Lorenzo's* losse;
That when the battel and the fight was done,
They knew not well whether they lost or wonne.   140

    Attic. This newes is worse then death; Happy were I
If any now could tell me he were dead;
Death is farre sweeter then captiuitie:
My deare *Lorenzo!* Was it thy desire
To goe to Warre, made thee forsake thy Father,
Countrie, Friends, Life, Libertie? and vndergoe
Death, or Capiuitie, or some disaster
That exceeds 'em both? Yet, howso'er,
Captaine, We thanke thy loue. Giue the reward
Was promis'd in the Proclamation.   150

    Capt. I'le not be nice in the refusall, Sir,
It is no wonder t'see a Souldier want:
All good wait on yee; may the Heauens be pleas'd
To make you happy in your long lost sonne.

    Attic. My comfort is, whether aliue or dead,
He brauely fought for Heauen and Christendome;
Such battels martyr men: their death's a life
Suruiuing all this worlds felicitie.
Lords, Where's *Leonida,* Our beautious child,
She's all the comfort we haue left Vs now;   160
She must not haue her libertie to match,
The Girle is wanton, coy, and fickle too:
How many Princes hath the froward Elfe
Set at debate, desiring but her loue?
What dangers may insue? But to preuent,
Nicanor, wee make you her Gardian:
Let her be Princely vs'd; but no accesse

---

    149 loue. Giue] loue; giue

By any to her presence, but by such
As wee shall send, or giue commandment for:
'Tis death to any other dares attempt it. 170
I heare, the Prince of Naples seekes her loue:
Shee shall not wed with that presumptuous Boy,
His father and Our selfe were still at oddes,
Nor shall He thinke Wee will submit to Him.
Certaine he knowes not of *Lisandro's* sute,
For if he had, he would a come himselfe,
Or sent Ambassadors to speake for him.
We'le giue his answer ere tomorrows Sunne
Shall reach to his Meridian, wretched state of Kings,
What end will follow where such woes begin? 180

Exeunt omnes. Manet
Nicanor *and* Scanfardoe.

Nican. Scanfardoe?
Scanf. My good Lord?
Nican. How lik'st thou this?
I am made Guardian of my owne harts blisse;
The Princesse is my Prisoner, I her Slaue;
I keepe her Body, but shee holds my Heart
Inuiron'd in a Chest of Adamant.
 Scanf. Is your Heart Iron?
 Nican. Steele, I thinke it is;
And like an Anuile hammerd by her words,
It sparkles fire that neuer can bee quencht, 190
But by the dew of her cœlestiall breath.
Oft haue I courted, bin reiected too;
Yet what of that? I'le trye her once agen.
What many Princes haue attempting fail'd,
I by accesse may purchase, that's my hope;
The King I'me sure affects mee; nothing then

---
178 tomorrows] to morrows
179 reach] retch
180 begin] begins
182 Nicanor] *Nicanor*   Scanfardoe.] *Scanfardoe.*
184 blisse;] G; ~,
185 Slaue;] G; ~,
189 like] G; liue
192 too;] G; ~,
196 mee;] G; ~,

Is wanting but her loue; that once obtain'd
Sicill is ours. *Scanfardoe!* if we win,
Thou shalt be Lord *Nicanor,* I the King.   *Exeunt.*

Scene. ii.
Enter Mysogenos *solus.*

Misog. By this, my thundering Booke is prest abroad.
I long to heare what a report it beares;
I know 't will startle all our Citie Dames,
Worse then the roring Lyons, or the sound
Of a huge double Canon; *Swetnams* name,
Will be more terrible in womens eares,
Then euer yet *Misogenysts* hath beene.

Enter Clowne.

Clown. Puffe, giue me some ayre,   10
I am almost stifled, puffe, Oh, my sides!
  Misog. From whence comm'st thou in such a puffing heate?
Hast thou been running for a wager, *Swash?*
Thou art horribly imbost. Where hast thou beene?
My life, he was haunted with some Spirit.
  Clown. A Spirit? I thinke all the Deuils in Hell,
Haue had a pinch at my hanches;
I haue beene among the Furies, the Furies:
A Pox on your Booke: I haue beene paid ifaith;
You haue set all the women in the Towne in an vprore. 20
  Misog. Why, what's the matter, *Swash?*
  Clown. Ne'r was poore *Swash,* so lasht, and pasht,
And crasht and dasht, as I haue beene;
Looke to your selfe, they're vp in armes for you.
  Misog. Why, Haue they weapons, *Swash?*
  Clown. Weapons, Sir, I, Ile be sworne they haue.

---

  197 loue;] G; ~,
  198 ours.] ~: *Scanfardoe!*] G; ~?
    2 abroad.] ~,
    3 beares;] ~,
    4 know 't will] know't will
    6 Canon;] ~,
    8 yet *Misogenysts*] yet in *Misogenysts*
   17 hanches;] G; ~,
   19 ifaith;] ~,
   23 beene;] G; ~,

And cutting ones, I felt the smart of 'em,
From the loines to the legs, from the head to th' hams,
From the Front to the foot, I haue not one free spot.
Oh, I can shew you, Sir, such Characters.   *Begins to strip.*   30
   Misog. What dost thou mean, man, wilt shame thy selfe?
   Clown. Why, here's none but you and I, Sir, is there?
   Misog. Good, good, ifaith. This was a braue Reuenge.
   Clown. If't be so good, would you had had't for me.
   Misog. And if I liue, I will make all the World
To hate, as I doe, this affliction, Woman.
   Clown. But we shall be afflicted in th'meane time.
Pray let's leaue this Land: if we stay heere,
We shall be torne a-pieces: would we had kept
In our owne Countrey, there w'are safe enough: 40
You might haue writ and raild your bellifull,
And few, or none would contradict you, Sir.
   Misog. Oh, but for one that writ against me, *Swash,*
Ide had a glorious Conquest in that Ile.
How my Bookes tooke effect! how greedily
The credulous people swallowed downe my hookes!
How rife debate sprang betwixt man and wife!
The little Infant that could hardly speake,
Would call his Mother Whore. O, it was rare!
   Clown. [*Aside.*] Oh, damn'd Rogue!   50
I stay but here, in hope, to see him hang'd,
And carrie newes to *England*; then I know,
The women there will neuer see me want,
For God he knows, I loue vm with my heart,
But dare not shew it for my very eares.
[*To Misogynos.*] What course, Sir, shall we take to hide our
   selues?
   Misog. The same we did at *Bristow,* Fencing Boy;
Oh 't is a fearefull name to Females, *Swash;*
I haue bought Foiles alreadie, set vp Bils,

---

   30 SD *Begins to strip.*]G; om.
   44 Ile.] ~,
   46 hookes!] ~∧
   52 *England;*] ~,
   58 *Swash;*] ~,

Hung vp my two-hand Sword, and chang'd my name: 60
Call me *Mysogenos*.

Enter Scanfardo.

Clown.   A sodden Nose.
Misog. *Mysogenos,* I say. Remember, *Swash;*
Heere comes a Gentleman.
I know him well; he serues a Noble Lord.
Seignior *Scanfardo,* happily encountred.
   Scanf. Thanks, my noble Gladiator, Doctor of Defence.
   Misog. A Master, Sir, of the most magnanimous Method of
Cudgell-cracking.
   Scanf. Ime glad I met with you.
I was now comming to be entred, Sir.   70
   Misog. That you shall presently. My Rapier, *Swash.*
Come, Sir, I'll enter you.
   Scanf.   What meane you, Sir?
   Misog. You say you would be entred; if you will,
Ile put you to the *Puncto* presently.
   Scanf. Your Scholler, Sir, I meane.
   Misog.   O welcome, Sir!
What, have you brought your Fees?
   Scanf.   Yes, Sir: what is't?
   Misog. Twentie *Piastros,* your admittance Sir,
And fiue, your quarteridge.
   Clown.   Besides Vshers Fees.
There goes a garnish and a breake-fast too.
   Scanf. Well, I'm content, there 'tis.   80
   Clown. Come when you will; find you *Piastros,* Sir,
And we'll find you crackt crownes.
   Misog. Booke him, my bold Vsher.
   Clown. That I will; your denomination, Seignior.
   Scanf. Seignior *Scanfardo, Della Sancta Cabrado.*
   Clown. Seig. Scan. *Della Sancta Cabrado?* a terrible name.

---

63 *Swash;*] G; ~,
63-64 *Swash;*/ Heere comes] G; Swash, heere/ comes
65 well;] ~,
73 entred;] G; ~,
75-76 Sir!/What,] G; Sir, What,
81 will;] ~,
84 will;] ~,

Misog. Giue me your hand, Scholer, so Ile cal you now.
Ile make you one of the Sonnes of Art.
Swash, giue my Scholer the Foyle.

Clown. Doe not take it in scorne; I haue gi'n many a good 90
Gentleman the Foyle, Sir.

Misog. I was going this morning to practise a young Duellist,
That shortly goes to fight at *Callis Sands.*
Come, Sir, to your guard.

Scanf. Not here in publike, I am a young beginner.
Come to my Chamber, Sir, Ile practise there.

Misog. Doe, and Ile teach you the very mysterie
of Fencing, that in a fortnight, you shall be able to
challenge any Scholer vnder the degree of a Prouost,
and in a quarter of a yeere, beat all the Fencers in 100
Germany. Our English Masters of this Noble Science
would ha' gi'n fortie pound to haue knowne that
tricke.

Scanf. Say you so, Sir? By this hand, I shall thinke my money
well bestowed then: but to tell you the truth, Sir, the reason I
would learne, is, because I am to bee married shortly: and they
say, Then or neuer, is the time for a man to get the mastery.

Misog. How, marry, Scholer? thou art not mad, I hope. Doe
you know what you doe?

Scanf. I know what I shall doe, Master, that's as good. 110

Misog. Doe you know what she is you are to marrie?

Scanf. A woman, I am sure a that.

Misog. No, she's a Deuill, Harpie, Cockatrice.

Scanf. And you were not my Master—

Misog. Scholer, be aduised, they are all most vile and wicked.

Scanf. How, Sir?

Misog. Dissemblers, the very curse of man, Monsters indeed.

Clown. That Ile be sworne they are, for I haue knowne some
of vm, that ha' deuoured you three Lordships, in Cullices and
Caudles before Break-fast. 120

Misog. And creatures the most imperfect: for looke yee, Sir,
Th'are nothing of themselues,

90-91 scorne; I] scorne, / I
103 Sir? By] Sir? / By
115 all most] all/Most

Onely patcht vp to coozen and gull men,
Borrowing their haire from one, complexions from another,
Nothing their own that's pleasing, all dissembled;
Not so much, but their very breath
Is sophisticated with Amber-pellets, and kissing causes.
Marry a woman, Scholer? thou vndergo'st an harder task,
Then those bold Spirits, that did vndertake
To steale the great *Turke* into Christendome. 130
A woman! she's an Angell at ten, a Saint at fifteene,
A Deuill at fortie, and a Witch at fourescore.
If you will marry, marry none of these:
Neither the faire, nor the foule; the rich, nor the poore;
The good, nor the bad.
  Scanf. Who should I marry then, Sir?
  Misog.   Marry none at all.
  Scanf. Proceeds this from Experience?
  Misog. From Reason, Sir, the Mistris of Experience.
Happy were man, had woman neuer bin.
Why did not Nature infuse the gift of Procreation 140
In man alone, without the helpe of woman,
Euen as we see one seed, produce another?
  Clown. Or as you see one Knaue make twentie, Master.
  Misog. Thou saist true, Swash: or why might not a man
Reuiue againe, like to the Elme and Oake?
  Clown. Many Logger-heads doe, Sir.
  Misog. When they are cut downe to the very roote,
Yet in short time you see, young branches spring againe.
  Clown. If 'twere so at Tyburne, what a fine companie of Crack-
ropes would spring vp then? 150
  Misog. Then we should ne'r be acquainted with the
deceitfull deuices of a womans crooked conditions, which
are so many, that if all the World were Paper; the Sea,
Inke; Trees and Plants, Pens; and euery man Clarkes,
Scribes, and Notaries: yet would all that Paper be scribled
ouer, the Inke wasted, Pens worne to the stumps, and all

---

    125 dissembled;] G; ~,
    153 Paper;] ~,   Inke;] ~,
    154 Pens;] ~,

the Scriueners wearie, before they could describe the hun-
dreth part of a womans wickednesse.

Scanf. Me thinks you are too generall: some, no doubt,
As many men, are bad: condemne not all for some.   160
What thinke you, Sir, of those that haue good wiues?
I hope, you will confesse a difference.

Misog. And Reason too: and here's the difference,
Those that haue good wiues, ride to Hell
Vpon ambling Hackneyes, and all the rest
Vpon trotting Iades to the Deuill.

Scanf. Is that the difference? Ile not marrie sure,
Ile rather turne Whore-master, and goe a-foot to the Deuill.

Clown. You'l hardly doe that, if you loue whoring, Sir.
For many lose a Legge in such seruice.   170

Scanf. But doe you heare, Sir? how long is't since you became
such a bitter Enemie to women?

Misog. Since I had wisdome. When I was a Foole,
I doted on such Follies, but now I haue left vm,
And doe vow to be the euerlasting scourge
To all their Sex: What the reason is,
Ile tell you, Sir, hereafter: reade but that,   *Handing his book.*
I haue arraign'd vm all, and painted forth
Those Furies to the life,
That all the World may know that doth it read,   180
I was a true Mysogenist indeed.   *Exeunt.*

Scene. iii.

Enter Iago, *and* Lorenzo *disguised.*

Iago. You haue not seene the Court then?
Loren.   Not as yet.
But I desire to obserue the Fashions there.
How doe you stile your King of Sicilie?

Iago. Men call him, Sir, The iust King *Atticus;*
And truly too: for with an equall Scale

---

168 Whore-master, and] Whore-master,/And
174-175 vm,/And] vm, and
175-176 scourge/To] scourge to
176-177 is,/Ile] is, Ile
177 SD *Handing his book.*] G; om.

He waighes the offences betwixt man and man;
He is not sooth'd with adulation,
Nor mou'd with teares, to wrest the course of Iustice
Into an vniust current, to oppresse   10
The Innocent; nor do's he make the Lawes
Punish the man, but in the man the cause.
Shall I in briefe giue you his Character?
   Loren. A thing I couet much.
   Iago.   Attend mee then.
His state is full of maiestie and grace,
Whose basis is true Pietie and Vertue,
Where, vnderneath a rich triumphant Arch,
That does resemble the Tribunall Seat,
Garded with Angels, borne vpon two Columnes,
Iustice and Clemencie, he sits inthron'd.   20
His subiects serue him freely, not perforce,
And doe obey him more for loue, then feare;
Being a King not of themselues alone,
And their estates, but their affections:
A soueraigntie that farre more safetie brings,
Then do's an Armie to the guard of Kings.
   Loren. You haue describ'd, Sir, such a worthy Prince,
That well I cannot say, who is most happie;
Either the King for hauing so good subiects,
Or else the subiects for so good a King.   30
But pray proceed.
   Iago.   The Heauens to crowne his ioy
With Immortalitie in his happie Issue
Sent him two Royall sonnes, of whom the eldest
Was the sweet Prince *Lusyppus.* Was! oh me,
That euer I should liue to say, he was:
He was, but is not now, for he is dead.
The yongest was *Lorenzo,* for his yeeres,
The pride and glory of Sicilians,
And miracle of Nature, whose aspect,
Euen like a Comet, did attract all eyes   40

---

   7 man;] G; ~,
   10-11 oppresse/The Innocent; nor] G; oppresse the Innocent,/Nor
   20 inthron'd.] ~,
   31 ioy] ~,

With admiration, wonder and amazement,
And he good Prince, is lost, or worse, I feare:
But for his Daughter faire *Leonida,*
Her Fame not able to be circumscrib'd
Within the bounds of Sicilie, hath gone
Beyond the Pirean Mountaines, and brought backe
The chiefe Italian Princes, but their Loues
Were quitted with contempt and crueltie:
And many of our braue Sicilian Youths
Haue sacrific'd their liues to her disdaine. 50
Now to preuent the like euent hereafter,
'Twas thought fit her libertie should be awhile restraind,
For which intent, his Highnesse hath elected
The Lord *Nicanor* for her Guardian,
Who, 'tis thought, shall after his decease,
Espouse the Princesse, and be heire of Sicill.
   Loren. You told me of a Prince, you said was lost,
Which you pronounc'd so feelingly, as if
It had beene your losse in particular.
   Iago. Oh, it was mine, and euery good mans else, 60
That is oblig'd to vertue and desert.
   Loren. See how Report is subiect to abuse.
I knew the Prince *Lorenzo.*
   Iago.   Did you, Sir?
   Loren. But neuer knew in him any one sparke
Of worth or merit, that might thus inflame
The zeale of your affection.
   Iago.   Traytor, thou lyest
Which I will proue eu'n to thy heart, thou ly'st,
I tell thee, thou hast committed such a sinne
Against his deare Report, that thy base life
Is farre too poore to expiate that wrong. 70
Sir, will you draw?
   Loren. Forbeare, incensed man. I doe applaud
Thy noble courage, and I tell you, Sir,
The Prince *Lorenzo* was a man I lou'd
As dearely as my selfe: but pray resolue me;
Does he liue or not?
   Iago.   He liues,

Act I, Scene iii 69

In our eternall memorie he liues: but otherwise,
It's the generall feare of Sicily,
That he is dead, or in Captiuitie.
For when *Don Iohn,* the Spanish Generall, 80
Went with an Armie 'gainst the cruell Turkes,
In that still memorable Battell of Lepanto,
Our braue *Lorenzo,* too too vent'rous,
There lost his life, or worse, his libertie.
　Loren. Hath not Time with his rude hand
Defac'd the Impression of his Effigies
In your memories yet?
　Iago.　　　　No, nor will euer be, so long
As worth shall be admir'd, and vertue loued.
　Loren. You know him, if you see him?　*Throws off disguise.*
　Iago. [*Kneets.*] My Lord *Lorenzo!*
　Loren.　　　　Rise, my worthy Friend, 90
I haue made proofe of thy vnfayned loue.
　Iago. Th' exceeding happinesse to see you well,
Is more then ioy can vtter: On my knees
I beg your pardon for th' vnciuill speech
My ignorant tongue committed.
　Loren. No, thus I'le be reueng'd.　　*Imbraces him.*
I know thou louest mee, and I must inioyne
Thy loue vnto an act of secresie,
Which you must not denie.
　Iago.　　　　Sir, I obey.
　Loren. Then thus it is, I must coniure your faith, 100
And priuacie in my arriuall yet,
For I intend a while in some disguise
To obserue the times and humors of the Court.
　Iago. How meanes your Grace? can you indure to see
The Court eclipst with clouds of discontent,
Your father mourne your absence, and all hearts
Ore-whelm'd with sorrow, and you present, Sir?
　Loren. Iago, I'me resolu'd:
Therefore what shape or humor I assume,
Take you no notice that I am the Prince. 110

---

　89 him?] ~.
　89 SD *Throws off disguise.*] om.

Iago. Sir, I consent,
And vow to your concealement.
　Loren. It is enough; my brother's dead, thou saist:
I haue some teares to spend vpon his Tombe;
We are the next vnto the Diadem,
That's the occasion I obscure my selfe.
Happie's that Prince, that ere he rules, shall know,
Where the chiefe errors of his State doe grow.　　　　*Exeunt.*

---

112 enough;] ~,
113 Tombe;] ~,

Act. II. [Scene. i.]

Enter Lisandro, *and* Loretta,
seuerall.

Loret. My Lord *Lisandro,* y'are met happily.
Lisan. Loretta! welcome, welcome as my life.
How fares my dearest Saint?
Loret. Like a distressed Prisoner, whose hard fate
Hath bard her from all ioy in losing you,
A torment which she counts insufferable.
Lisan. This separation, like the stroke of death,
Makes a diuorce betwixt my soule and mee; 10
For how can I liue without her
In whom my life subsists?
For neuer did the Load-stone more respect
The Northerne Pole, by natures kind instinct,
Then my affections truly sympathize
With her, the Starre of my felicitie.
Loret. Therefore shee prayes you, henceforth to desist,
Respecting your owne safetie: Worthie Prince,
The times are troublesome and dangerous:
As for her selfe, she's arm'd to vndergoe 20
All malice that for you they can inflict.
Lisan. Oh my *Loretta!* thou appli'st a balme
Worse then the wound it selfe: It is impossible
For me to liue at all but in her sight.
But was this all shee said,
That I should leaue her? Death could not ha' spoke
A word more fatall to my soule and mee:
Let her inioyne mee to some other taske,
Tho it were greater then the sonne of *Ioue*
Did for his Step-dame *Iuno* euer act: 30

---
29 *Ioue*] Ioue

Let it be any thing, so I may not leaue
Her sweet societie.
    Loret.   Then, here my Lord, read this. *Gives him letter.*
    Lisan. I kisse thee for her sake, whose beautious hand
Hath here inclos'd so mild and sweet a doome.
See what a negatiue command shee hath
Impos'd vpon my sloth to visit her,
As if she taxed my neglect so long:
But pardon, deare *Leonida,* I come
To intimate thy fauor for my stay,
Tho thou wert garded with an host of men.   40
But how?
I must disguise me in some other shape,
For this is noted, and too full of danger.
Loretta, Who's admitted best accesse
Vnto thy Lady?
    Loret.   Frier *Anthonie,*
Her Graces Confessor.
    Lisan. As I could wish: I know the Frier well;
I must assume that shape; It is the best:
Loretta, weare this Iewell for my sake;   *She hesitates.*
Nay, prethee take it, not as recompence,   50
But as a token of that future good
Shall crowne thy merits, with such height and honour,
Fortune shall be asham'd, and held a Foole,
To suffer poore desert to ouer-match her.   *Exit* Lisandro.
    Loret. [*Calls after him.*] I humbly thanke your Grace:
Why, here's a gift
Able to make a Saint turne Oratrix,
And pleade 'gainst Chastitie: I must confesse,
Lisandro is a Noble Gentleman, and has good gifts,
And is, indeed, gracious with my Ladie: Yet for all
that, wee poore Gentlewomen, that haue no other fortunes   60
but our attendance, must now and then make the best vse
of our places: wee haue president, and very lately too.
But who comes here? my Lord *Nicanor?*

---

    32 SD *Gives him letter.*] om.
    49 SD *She hesitates.*] om.
    58 has] ha's

Enter Nicanor.

Here's another Client—
I must deuise some quaint deuice for him,
To delude his frostie apprehension—
Oh I ha't.
    Nican. Loretta, how is't, wench? How thriues
My suit, ha? Hast broke with thy Lady yet?   70
    Loret. [*Aside.*] He takes me for a Shee-Broker, but I'le fit him:
[*To* Nicanor.] I haue my Lord, but find her so obdure,
That when I speake, she turnes away her eare,
As if her mind were fixt on something else.
The other day, finding her Grace alone,
I came and mou'd your suit; told her how deare
She stood in your affection; and protested,
You lou'd her more then all the World beside.
    Nican. Good, good: proceed.
    Loret.   At this she answer'd not a word,
But kept her eye still fixt vpon me;   80
Then I begun agen, and told her Grace
(As from my selfe) how much your Honour
Had merited her fauour by desert;
How great you stood ith' generall eye of all,
As one selected by the King her Father,
(Since Prince *Lorenzo's* death) to personate
The King of Sicill after his decease.
    Nican. Excellent good i'faith. Then what said shee?
    Loret. At this, I might perceiue her colour change
From red to pale, and then to red againe,   90
As if disdaine and rage had faintly stroue
In her confused brest for victorie.
At length, hauing recal'd her spirits,
She broke forth into these words; What, wilt thou
Conspire with youth and frailtie, to inforce
The rule of my affection 'gainst my will?
Tho' my body be confin'd his prisoner,

    65-66 Client—/I] Client—I
    66-67 him,/To] him, to
    69-70 thriues/My] thriues my
    85 As] And

Yet my mind is free. With that, shee charg'd mee
That I neuer should hereafter vrge your suit;
And this was all the comfort that I could 100
From her with all my diligence attaine.
    Nican. Cold comfort, Wench, but 'tis the generall fault
Of women all, to make shew of dislike
To those they most affect: and in that hope
Thou shalt to her againe: No Citie
Euer yeelded at first skirmish. Before,
You came but to a parley, thou shalt now
Giue an assault: There's nothing batters more
A womans resolution, then rich gifts;
Then goe, *Loretta.*
    Loret.   'Las, my Lord, you know— 110
    Nican. Feare nothing, Wench, giue her this chaine of pearle,
With it my selfe.
    Loret. My Lord, I'le see what I can doe with her,
But—
    Nican. What, *Loretta?* Oh, you looke for a fee:
Here, take this Gold: And if thou canst preuaile,
(Harke in thine eare) When I am King—
    Loret. I thanke your Lordship: Ha, ha, ha—   *Exit* Loretta.
    Nican. This womans weaknesse was wel wrought vpon,
Her words may take effect: 'Tis often seene 120
That women are like Diamonds; nothing cut so soone
As their owne powder: yet there is one more
Will make a happy second,
Frier *Anthonie* her Confessor; such men as hee
Can preuaile much with credulous Penitents
In causes of perswasion. Hoe, within?

                Enter Scanfardo.

    Scanf. Your Lordship call?
    Nican.   Bid Frier *Anthonie*
Come visit mee with all speed possible.
                Exit Scanfardo.
I could not thinke vpon a better Agent. 130

---

    127 Scanfardo.] Seruant.
    129 SD *Exit* Scanfardo.] om.

Their seeming sanctitie makes all their acts
Sauour of Truth, Religion, Pietie,
And proue that loue's a heauenly Charitie,
Without which there's no safetie. Here he comes.

Enter Lisandro *like a Frier.*

Lisan. The benediction of the blessed Saints
Attend your honour.
   Nican.   Welcome, holy Frier.
   Lisan. And crowne your wishes to your hearts desire.
   Nican. Amen, *Anthonio,*
I'le say Amen to that; but yet the meanes   140
To make mee happy, lies within thy power.
   Lisan. Your Honour may command mee.
   Nican.   Then 'tis thus;
Thou know'st with what a generall consent
Of all Sicilia I was prelected
By my dread Soueraigne, to espouse the faire
Yet fond *Leonida;* granting me for dower
The Crowne of Sicil, after his decease.
   Lisan. I hope, my Lord, there's none dares question that.
   Nican. To which intent, how many hopefull Princes
Haue beene non-suted, onely for my sake?   150
And to preuent all meanes of their accesse,
Establish'd mee her Guardian: Now, the Princesse,
Although I haue her Person, yet her Heart
I find estrang'd from mee, and all my loue
Is quitted with contempt.
   Lisan.   The Heauens forbid.
   Nican. It is forbidden both by Heauen and Earth,
And yet Shee do's it; and thou know'st then, Frier,
My hopes are frustrate. Therefore (holy Man)
Thou art her Counsel-Closet, her Confessor,
Of reuerend opinion with the Princesse.   160
   Lisan. I doe conceiue your Honour.
   Nican.   Be my Orator.
   Lisan. In what I may, my Lord.
   Nican.   If thou preuail'st,

I'le make thee Metropolitane of Sicil.
   Lisan. It shall be all my care.
   Nican.   Then farewell, Father.   *Exit* Nicanor.
   Lisan. All my Prayers attend yee.
So, here's the fence throwne open; now my way
Is made before mee: Godamercy Cowle;
It is no maruell tho' the credulous World
Thought themselues safe from danger, when they were
Inuested with this habit, 'tis the best,   170
To couer, or to gaine a free accesse,
That can be possible in any proiect.
How finely I haue guld my Politician,
That couets Loue, onely to gaine a Crowne!
But if my Loue proue constant, Ile withstand
All his desires with a more powerful hand.   *Exit.*

[Scene. ii.]

Enter Leonida *and* Loretta.

   Leon. Tell me, *Loretta,* Art thou sure 'twas he?
   Loret. Madame, I liue not else.
   Leon.   Thou do'st delude
My feares with fond impossibilities:
Prethee resolue me truly, I do long
Most infinitely.
   Loret.   Not a syllable more now,
And it would saue your life: not be beleeu'd!
   Leon. Nay, sweet *Loretta.* Troth, I doe beleeue thee.
   Loret. Discredited!
I could fight with any liuing creature   10
In this quarrell 'tis so iust.
   Leon.   Haue I deseru'd
No more respect, then to be trifled thus?

---

     174 Crowne!] G; ~?
       7 it would] G; 'twould   be beleeu'd!] be-beleeu'd?
       8 *Loretta.* Troth,] *Loretta./*Troth,
       9 Discredited!] ~?
     10 creature₍ₐ₎] ~,
     11 quarrell,] quarrell

Come, prethee tell me.
Loret.   Yes! to delude
Your feares with fond impossibilities!
   Leon. Nay, now thou tortur'st me.
   Loret.   Well, I haue done.
But leaue your sighes, your heigh-ho's, and ay-me's:
For I haue newes will warme you like the Sunne,
And make you open like the Marigold.
   Leon. Why, now thou rauish'st me.
   Loret. I heard you not cry out yet.   20
   Leon. Thou takest such a delight in crossing me.
   Loret. 'Faith, now you talke of Crosses, Ile tell you,
You haue chosen a Husband, so handsome, so complete,
As if he had beene pickt out of the Christ-Crosse row.
   Leon. As how, I prethee?
   Loret.   Why, Madame, thus:
Ille begin with A. and so proceed to the latter end of the
Alphabet, comparing his good parts thus: for A. hee is
Amiable, Bountifull, Courteous, Diligent, Eloquent, Faith-
full, Gracious, Humble, Iouiall, Kind, Louing, Magnani-
mous, Noble, Patient, Quiet, Royall, Secret, Trustie,   30
Vigilant, Wittie, and
Xceeding Youthfull. Now for Z, he's zealous:
So I conclude, pray God hee bee not Iealous.
   Leon. An excellent obseruation.
   Loret. Who doe you think's in loue with you?
The old Dragon *Nicanor,* that watches the fruit of your
Hesperides.
   Leon. Oh, that newes is stale.
   Loret. He met me but iust now, and would needs know,
What returne I had made of his Aduenture.   40
But I deuised such a Tale for my old Marchant,
Able to make a Bankrout at report,
But he notwithstanding fraughts me agen,
With that he was not able, but with this,

---

      13 Yes!] ~?
      14 impossibilities!] ~?
      24 pickt out] pickt/Out
      31-32 and/Xceeding] and Xceeding
      32-33 zealous:/So] zealous:so
      39 me but] G; ˄ but

This Chaine of Pearle.
  Leon. Prethee, away with it, Ile not be chain'd to him.
  Loret. Faith, and 'tis true, a Chaine is the worst Gift a Louer can send his Mistris, 'tis such an Embleme of bondage hereafter. Who's that?

                    Enter Lisandro.   50

  Leon. Father.
  Lisan. How fares my worthy Daughter?
  Leon.   Eu'n as one
Deuoted vnto sorrow, griefe and mone.
  Lisan. Then I must blame you, Ladie, you doe ill,
To blast those Rosiall blossomes. Will you kill
This gift of Nature, Beautie in the prime?
  Leon. Father, I vnderstand not what you say:
The other day you talkt of Penitence,
Commended Patience, Sorrow and Contrition,
As Antidotes against the soules decay: 60
And now, me thinkes, you speake of no such thing.
  Lisan. Mistake me not, deare Daughter, I spake then,
Onely to mortifie the sinfull minde,
But now I come with comfort, to restore
Your fainting spirits that were grieu'd before:
But Daughter, I must chide you.
  Leon.   Father, why?
  Lisan. For your neglect, and too much crueltie
To one that dearely loues you.
  Leon. Whom in the name of wonder?
  Loret.   On my life,
This Frier's made an agent in my suit.   70
  Lisan. The hope of Sicill, Map of true Nobilitie,
Patterne of Wisdome, Grace and Grauitie.
  Leon. You prayse him highly, has he ne'r a name?
  Lisan. Yes, 'tis my Lord *Nicanor.*
  Leon.   Oh, is't he?
His gray head shewes his wisdomes grauitie:

---

47 Gift a] Gift/A
48 Embleme of] Embleme/Of
73 has] ha's
74 'tis] G; is't

And are you made his Agent,
His Aduocate, to play the spokesman? Fie.
    Lisan. Daughter, this is a worke of Charitie,
A holy action to combine in one:
Two different hearts in holy Vnion.
    Leon.   Frier, no more.   80
I doe not like of these perswasions,
Either ya're not the same you seeme to be,
Or all your Actions are Hypocrisie;
My Faith is past alreadie, and my heart
Ingag'd vnto a farre more worthy man:
Lisandro is the Prince my loue hath wonne.
    Lisan. Then here the Frier concludes: my taske is done.

                            Throws off disguise.

    Leon. Lisandro, my deare Loue!
    Lisan.   The same, sweet Princesse.
    Leon. Oh, you were too aduentrous, dearest Loue,   90
What made you vndertake this hard attempt?
    Lisan. Your loue, sweet Lady, that makes all things easie.
    Leon. Oh, I am made immortall with thy sight:
Here let me euer liue: I feare not now
The worst that Fate or Malice can afflict:
I haue enough, hauing thy companie.
    Linsan. And when I leaue to loue you, vertuous Madame,
Vpon that minute, let me leaue to liue,
That loue and life may both expire together.
    Loret. Come, leaue your prating and protesting,   100
And get you both in, and be naught awhile.
'Tis dangerous talking here in publike.
Good Frier, look my Ladie dye no Nun.

                        Exit Leonida *and* Lisandro.

Heigho! now could I wish my Sweet-heart
Heere too, I feele such a tickling, somewhere
About me: if he were here now, I would

---

    83 Hypocrisie;] G; ~,
    88 SD *Throws off disguise.*] om.
    92 Lady, that] G2; Lady,/That
    102 publike.] ~,

Neuer cast such an vnwilling deniall vpon him
As I haue done, hauing so good a president as I haue.

Enter Scanfardo.   110

But stay, who's this? As true as I liue, 'tis he.
Oh, sweet Rogue, thou art come in the happiest minute.
   Scanf. Am I, *Loretta?* Masse, I like that well.
What, all alone? I like that better too.
But where's the Princesse?
   Loret.   Oh, she's safe enough!
   Scanf. Is she indeed?   I like that best of all.
   Loret. And so do's shee, I warrant yee,
Or any woman else, that's in her Case: ha, ha, ha!
   Scanf. There's something in the wind now, that you laugh at.
   Loret. Nothing indeed, sweet Loue: but ha, ha!   120
I laugh at an odde Iest.
   Scanf.   Come, I must know't.
   Loret. 'Deed but you must not.
   Scanf. Why? Dare you not trust me?
   Loret.   Yes, I dare:
But as you are a man, reueale it not.
   Scanf. In troth, Ime angry, that you should mistrust me.
   Loret. The Frier, the Frier: ha, ha, ha!
He that the Lord imploy'd to be his Agent,
Who doe you thinke it was?
   Scanf.   Father *Anthonie,* wast not?
   Loret. The Deuill it was: no faith, it was, ha, ha, ha!
It was no other, then *Lisandro* Prince of *Naples,*   130
That stole to my Lady in that Habit,
And guld your Lord most palpably.
   Scanf. Is't possible? And where are they now?
   Loret. Why? faith th'are eu'n at. Ha, ha, ha, ha!
But good Sweet-heart, be silent.
   Scanf. Not a syllable I: it was a bold attempt,

---

    110 SD *Enter* Scanfardo.] *follows line* 112 *in* Q
    111 this? As] this?/As
    112 come in] come/In
    123-124 dare:/But as] dare: but/As
    129 faith, it] faith,/It
    133 possible? And] possible?/And
    134 at. Ha,] at,/Ha,

Knowing 'twas death, if but discouered once.
But come, Sweet-heart, weele eu'n doe,
As our betters haue done before vs,
The example is easly followed, 140
Hauing so good a Schoole-mistris.
Shall we to bed?
   Loret.   Fye, seruant, how you talke?
Troth you are to blame, to offer to assault
The chastitie of any Gentlewoman,
Vpon aduantage.
   Scanf. Pox, leaue this forc'd modesty: for by this hand,
I must enioy you now before we part.
   Loret. I haue so farre ingag'd my selfe, you know,
'Tis now vaine to resist.
   Scanf. Why, now I like thee well. Where shall we meet? 150
   Loret. In the with-drawing Chamber, there I lye.
   Scanf. Goe then, Ile follow.
   Loret.   Ile put out the light.
   Scanf. No matter, I shall find the way i' the darke.

                                                       Exit Loretta.

Here was a strange discouerie but indeed,
What will not women blab to those they loue?
I am very loth to leaue my sport tonight,
And yet more loth to lose that rich reward
My Lord will giue for this discouerie,
Chiefly to be reueng'd vpon his riuall: 160
Ile not forsake it, Venerie is sweet.
But he that has good store of gold and wealth,
May haue it at command, and not by stealth.   *Exit.*

[Scene. iii.]

Enter Lisandro *and* Leonida.

   Lisan. 'Tis late, dear Loue.
   Leon.   You shall not part from me,
Good sooth, you shall not. Frier *Anthonie,*
You say, is faithfull: for *Loretta's* truth

---

   150 well. Where] well./Where
   154 *Exit* Loretta.] om.
   157 tonight] to night

82 Swetnam the Woman-hater

I dare ingage my life.
   Lisan.   Why, so you doe;
Should she proue false, both yours and mine, you know,
Are forfeit to the Law.
   Leon.   You are secure.
Mistrust not then: true loue is void of feare.
No danger can afflict a constant mind.   10
This is no durance, no imprisonment,
Rather a Paradise in ioying thee:
My libertie alone consists in thee.
   Lisan. That is the reason, Ime so iealous, Sweet,
Since in my freedome both our liues remaine.
As for my selfe, what perill could be thought,
I would not vndergoe to gaine your loue?
Were it to scale the flaming Ætna's top:
Whose sulphurous smoke kils with infection,
Cut through the Northerne Seas, or shoote the Gulfe?   20
Or—
   Leon. I doe beleeue thee, Sweet.
   Lisan.   But yet this houre
Is not frequented by your Confessor,
There lyes the danger.
   Leon. I ha' confest to thee, from morne till night,
From night till morne againe, all my transgression.
   Lisan. Were I your Confessor, I know you would
Both sinne, and be confest.
   Nican. [*From without.*] Breake ope the doore.
   Lisan. By Heauen, we are betrai'd.
   Leon.   Oh my deare Loue.
   Lisan. My thoughts presag'd as much. What shall we doe?   30

Enter Nicanor *and a Guard.*

   Leon. Do not resist, *Lisandro,* stand: the worst,
We can but dye.
Oh, this *Loretta,* false, inhumane wretch!
   Nican. Lay hands vpon them both. Is't so indeed?

    23-24 Confessor,/There] G; Confessor, there
    26/27 ₐ] SD *Enter* Nicanor.
    30 much. What] G; much./What

Is this the zeale of your Confession?
I feare, death giues the absolution.
    Leon. Hence, doting Foole, more welcome far is death,
Then to bee linkt to Ages Leprosie. *Exeunt.*
    Nican. Beare vm away into their seuerall Wards.   40
Let them be guarded strongly, till such time
I shall acquaint my Soueraigne with this Plot.
Rather then lose the Royall Dignitie,
Ile striue to ruine a whole Progenie. *Exit.*

Act. III. [Scene. i.]

Enter Atticvs, Iago, Nicanor, *two Iudges,
Notarie, and Attendants.*

Attic. How full of troubles is the state of Kings,
Abroad, with Foes, at home, with faithlesse Friends,
Within with cares, without, a thousand feares!
Yet all summ'd vp together, doth not make
Such an impression in our troubled thoughts,
As this one Act of disobedience
In our own Issue.
   Iago.   Gracious Soueraigne,
Yet for that high respect, be fauourable: 10
She is your Daughter.
   1. Iudge.   And the onely hope
Of all Sicilie, since *Lorenzo's* losse.
   Attic. Bring to the Barre the Prisoners: this offence
Hath lost in vs a Father and a Friend,
And cals for Iustice from vs, as a King:
Yet thinke not, Lords, but 'tis with griefe of mind,
Nor can a Father easly forget
A Daughter whom hee once so dearely lou'd:
Yet we had rather become Issulesse,
Then leaue it noted to Posteritie,   20
An Act of such Iniustice.
   2. Iudge.   Yet, dread Liege,
Oh, doe not too much aggrauate the crime,
Rather impute it to their childish loue.
   Attic. To loue, my Lords? if that were lowable,

---
    4 Abroad,] ~∧
    5 feares!] G; ~?
    9-11 Soueraigne,/Yet . . . respect, be fauourable:/She] G; Soueraigne, yet . . . respect,/Be fauourable: she
    17-18 forget/A Daughter whom] G; forget a Daughter,/Whom

What Act so vile, but might be so excus'd?
The Murderer, that sheddeth guiltlesse bloud,
Might plead, it was for loue of his Reuenge,
The Felon likewise might excuse his theft,
With loue of money, and the Traytor too
Might say, It was for loue of Soueraigntie.   30
And indeed, all offenders so might plead.   *A Barre.*
Therefore, my Lords, you that sit here to Iudge,
Let all respect of persons be forgot,
And deale vprightly, that you may resemble
The highest Iudge, whose seat on Earth you hold:
And for you know, the Lawes of Sicilie
Forbid to punish two, for one offence,
Let your care be to find the principall,
The *Primus Motor* that begun the cause;
For the effect (you see) is but the issue   40
That one of them may worthily receiue
Deserued death; the other, may be sent
(As lesse offending) into banishment.   *Exit King.*

Enter Lisandro, *and* Leonida.
The Prisoners brought to the Barre by a Gard.

   1. *Iudge.* Th' offence wherewith you both stand tax'd withall,
Appeares so manifest in grosse, that now
We need not question all particulars
In publique here: but yet your triall shall
Be honourable, as your Persons were   50
Before this blacke Impression. Therefore say,
Which of you two begun th'occasion,
By any meanes, direct or indirect?
And answer truely, as you looke for grace.
   Lisan. 'Twas I, my honour'd Lords.
   Leon.   My Lords, 'twas I.
   Lisan. Let not this honourable Court be swaid
By false suggestions; that the fault was mine,
Appeares as manifest as mid-dayes Sunne,
'Twas I that first attempted, su'd, and prai'd,
Vs'd all the subtile engins Art could inuent,   60

---

49 here: but yet] G; here: yet

Or Nature yeeld, to force affection,
Onely to gaine the royall Princesse loue;
For what can Women aboue weakenesse act?
Or, what Fort's so strong, but yeelds at length
To a continued siege?
Th' attempt, I knew, was hard and dangerous:
Therefore more honourable in the conquest;
Which ere I would haue left, I would ha' past
More dangers then ere *Iason* vnder-went.
Then, since you see (my Lords) the guilt was mine,   70
Pardon the Princesse, Mee to death resigne.
  Leon. Pardon (my Lords) *Lisandro,* let me dye:
If euer you'le performe an act of iustice
Shall make you truely famous, doe it here,
Here vpon me; the guilt alone is mine:
'Twas this alluring face, and tempting smiles,
That drew on his affections. Say that Hee
Did first commence the suit; the fault was mine
In yeelding to it; 'Tis a greater shame
For women to consent, then men to aske: 80
And yet, before he spoke, I had ingag'd
My heart and loue to him, vnask'd, vnpraid;
And then (you know) how soone our eyes discouers
The true affection that we beare our Louers:
Then since the guilt alone remaines in Mee,
Let me be iudg'd, and set *Lisandro* free.
  2. Iudge. This knot is intricate.
  Lisan.   'Tis fallacie.
Who can alledge one Article 'gainst her?
Th' offence was, breaking of the Kings command,
That none, on paine of death, should visit her,   90
Vnlesse appoynted by the King himselfe;
And that alone was mine: 'Twas my deuice;
I tooke the borrowed shape; I broke the Law,
And I must suffer for't: Then doe not wrong
Her spotlesse Chastitie.
  1. Iudge.   How, Chastitie?

---

95 SD *1. Iudge.*] *4. Iudge.*

Lisan. If any here conceiue her otherwise,
That very thought will damne him: She's as chaste
As ere your Mothers in their cradles were,
For any act committed.
   2. *Iudge.*   Harder still.
   1. *Iudge.* A confused Labyrinth: we shal ne'r wind out.   100
   Leon. My Lords, beleeue him not; the guilt lies here:
'Twas I that sent him that deluding shape,
In which he got admittance; The offence
Rests onely here: And therefore (good my Lords)
Let the condemning sentence passe on mee;
Or else, I will protest to all the world,
You are vniust; And take my death vpon't.
   Lisan. Fie, Madam, how you wrong your innocence!
And seeming (Lady) to be pittifull
To mee, you are most cruell; for my life   110
Should be a willing sacrifice to death,
To expiate the guilt of my offence.
Remember what continuall paines I tooke,
By messages, intreaties, gifts, and prayers,
To win your fauour, deare *Leonida.*
Iustice in this will be Impietie,
Vnlesse it here be shew'd. I beg it may
   Leon. I beg against him: He is innocent;
The fact alone was mine: I was the first,
The middle, and the end;   120
And Iustice here must end,
Or 'tis iniustice.

                  Enter King.

Attic.   Is the sentence giuen?
   2. *Iudge.* Not yet, my Lord: We are as far to seeke,
In the true knowledge of the prime Offender,
As at the first; for they plead guilty both;
Both striue to aggrauate their owne offence,
And Both excuse each other. On our liues,
We cannot yet determine where's the cause.

---
    97 him: She's] him:/She's
  107 vniust; And] G; vniust;/And

Attic. It is impossible 130
That sacred Iustice should be hudwink't still,
Though she be falsly painted so; Her eyes
Are cleare, and so perspicuous, that no cryme
Can maske it selfe in any borrowed shape,
But shee'le discouer it. Let vm be returnd
Backe to their seuerall Wards, till we deuise
Some better course for the discouery.
    Nican. Dread Soueraigne, I know no better way,
Then to assay by torture, to inforce
A free confession, seuerall, one from other: 140
For though they now, out of affection,
Plead their owne guilt, as if they feard not death;
Yet, when they feele him sting once, then the care
Of life, and safetie, will discouer all.
    Iago. My Lord *Nicanor,* this is ill aduis'd,
Sauoring too much of force and tyrannie.
Is't fit that Princes should subiect themselues
To any tortures, such as are prepared
For base Offendors? 'Tis ignobly done,
So to incense the King.
    Nican.   How, Sir!
    Iago.   Eu'n so: 150
You shew a proud aspiring mind, my Lord,
After a Kingdome, that would ruinate
Two royall Louers for so small a fact:
But, Marke my words, Nicanor; Ere the Crowne
Impale thy Temples by Her timelesse end,
Mine and fiue thousand liues shall all expire.
    Nican. I wey thy words not this. [*Snaps fingers.*]
    Iago.   Nor I thy frowne;
I'le incense one, shall quickly pull you downe.   *Exit.*
    Attic. How's your opinion then, to search it out?
    1. *Iudge.* My Liege, we know no better way then this, 160
Let there be publique Proclamation made
Throughout the Kingdome, that there may be found
Two Aduocates, to plead this difference

---

    159 then, to] then,/To

In publique disputation, Man and Woman,
The wisest, and the best experienc'd
That can be found, or heard of in the Land:
Or any such will proffer of themselues
To vndertake the plea; For, questionlesse,
None are so impudent to vndergoe
So great a controuersie, except those   170
That know themselues sufficient.
 Attic.   Wee are pleas'd.
See it effected with all the speed you can:
The charge be yours, my Lord. Dissolue the Court.
          Exeunt Omnes.

[Scene. ii.]

Enter Iago *and* Lorenzo, *disguised like an Amazon.*

 Loren. Has my poore Sister then withstood a triall?
 Iago. I, and behau'd her selfe
Most royall, and discreetly: Insomuch,
Shee put the Iudges to non-plus, Sir;
Defending and excusing eythers cause,
Vntill *Nicanor,* with his kind aduice,
Desir'd the King they might be tortured,
To see if that would force confession.   10
 Loren. Was he the onely Tyrant? Well, ere long
It may be in Our power to quittance him.
I'me glad I know the Serpents subtiltie.
But how concluded they?
 Iago.   I was so vext,
I could not stay a full conclusion.
The Prisoners were dismist before I came:
But how they did determine afterwards,
I long to heare. But what intends your Grace
In this disguise?
 Loren.   To visit the sicke Court,
And free my Sister from captiuitie,   20
With that good Prince *Lisandro.*

Enter Misogynos *and* Scanfardo *conversing.*

Misog. [*Not noticing* Iago *and* Lorenzo.] A Woman!
Why the more I thinke of their wickednesse,
The more incomprehensible I find it;
For they are, coozening, cologuing, vngratefull, deceitful,
Wauering, waspish, light, toyish, proud, sullen,
Discourteous, cruell, vnconstant; and what not?
Yet, they were created, and by nature formed,
And therefore of all men to be auoyded.

    Loren. [*To one side.*] Oh impious conclusion! What is hee?   30
    Iago. I ne'r had conuersation with him yet;
But (by report) I'le tell you, He's a man,
Who's breeding has beene like the Scarrabee,
Altogether vpon the excrement of the time;
And being swolne with poysonous vapors,
He breakes wind in publique, to blast the
Reputation of all Women; His acquaintance
Has bin altogether amongst Whores and Bawds,
And therefore speakes but in's owne element.
His owne vnworthie foule deformitie,   40
Because no Female can affect the same,
Begets in him despaire; and despaire, enuie.
He cares not to defame their very soules,
But that he's of the Turkes opinion: They haue none.
He is the Viper, that not onely gnawes
Vpon his Mothers fame, but seekes to eat
Thorow all Womens reputations.

    Loren. Is't possible! that Sicilie should breed
Such a degenerate Monster, shame of men?
    Iago. Blame not your Countrie, he's an Englishman.   50
    Loren. I will not see the glories of that Sexe
Be-spawld by such a dogged Humorist,
And passe vnpunisht.
    Iago.   What intends your Grace?
    Loren. To vndertake this iust and honest quarrell,
In the defence of Vertue, till I haue

---

    22 SD *conversing.*] om.

Seuerely punisht his opprobrious word,
Committed against Women, who's iust fame
Merits an Angels Pen to register.
    Scanf. [*To* Misogynos.] Sir, you haue alter'd me, I thanke
you for't.
    Misog. Oh! they are all the very pits of Sin,   60
Which men, for want of wisdome, fall into.
    Scanf. I see it, Sir, and will proclaime as much. *Exit* Scanfardo.
    Loren. Leaue me, *Iago.*
    Iago.   I'me gone, sweet Prince.   *Exit* Iago.
    Loren. [*To* Misogenos.] Tell me, thou iangling Mastiffe, with
what feare
Dar'st thou behold that too much wronged Sex,
Whose Vertues thou hast basely slander'd?
    Misog. Ha, ha, ha.
    Loren. Laugh'st thou, inhumane wretch? By my best hope,
But that thy malice hath deseru'd reuenge
More infamous, and publique, then to fall   70
By me in priuate, I would hew thy flesh
Smaller then Attomes.
    Misog. What haue we here? A Woman rampant? ha!
Tempt me not, Syren, lest thou does inuoke
A Furie worse then Woman.
    Loren.   Hellish Fiend,
How dar'st thou vtter such blasphemous words,
In the contempt of Women, whose deserts
Thy dunghill basenesse neuer could discerne?
Assure thy selfe, thy malice shall be plagu'd
Seuerely, as in iustice thou deseru'st.   80
    Misog. I wey not your threats this [*Snaps fingers.*]; spit out
your poysons,
Till your gals doe burst, I will oppose you all;
I cannot flatter, I: nor will I fawne
To gaine a fauor; Prayse the hand and foot,
And sweare your face is Angel-like, and lye
Most grosly. No, I will not do't.

---

    64 SD *Exit* Iago.] om.
    73 What͵] ~,   here? A] here/A

But when I come, it shall be in a storme,
To terrifie you all, that you shall quake
To heare my name resounding in your eares:
And Fortune, if thou be'st a deitie, 90
Giue me but opportunitie, that I
May all the follies of your Sex declare,
That henceforth Men of Women may beware.

Enter a Herald with a Proclamation, a Trumpet before him, a great rabble of men following him.

Herald. Atticus, King of Sicilia, to all his louing Subject sendeth greeting: Whereas there is a doubtfull question to be decided in publique disputation, which concernes the honour of all men in generall, that is to say, Whether the Man or the Woman in loue, stand guilty 100 of the greatest offence: Know therefore, if that any man, of what estate or condition soeuer, will vndertake to defend the equitie of men, against the false imputations of women, let vm repayre to the Court, they shall be honourably entertayned, graciously admitted, and well rewarded. *God saue the King.*

Omnes. Heauen preserue his Grace.

Misog. Fortune, I doe adore thee for this newes:
Why, here's the thing I lookt for; 'tis a prize
Will make me euer famous. *Herald,* stay, 110
I will maintaine the Challenge, and approue
That women are first tempters vnto loue.
I'le blazon forth their colours in such sort,
Shall make their painted cheekes looke red, for vm
To haue them noted theirs, that all may know
That women onely are the cause of woe.

Omnes. A Champion, a Champion! *Exeunt.*

Enter Loretta *with a Proclamation, and as many Women as may be, with a Trumpet afore them.*

Loret. Aurelia, Queene, by the especiall priuiledge of 120
the Maiestie of Sicilia, to all Ladies, gentle and others,

105-106 rewarded. *God*] rewarded./*God*
118 SD Loretta] *a Woman*

of the Female Sex, sends greeting: Whereas there is a
question to be decided in publike disputation before an
Honourable Assembly of both parts, that is, whether the
man or the woman in loue commit the greatest offence, by
giuing the first and principall occasion of sinning: therefore know, that if any woman will vndertake to defend
the innocency of women, against the false imputations
of detracting men, let her repair to the Court, shee
shall bee honourably entertayned, graciously admitted, and
well rewarded. *God saue the Queene.* 130
  Omnes. Heauens preserue her.
  Loren. I doe accept it, tis a cause so iust,
In equitie and vertue, in defence
Of wronged women, whose distressed fames
Lye buried in contempt, whose Champion
I doe professe my selfe, and doe desire
No greater glorie, then to haue that name.
What woman can indure to heare the Wrongs,
Slanders, Reproches, and base Forgeries, 140
That baser men vaunt forth, to dimme the rayes
Of our weake tender Sex? But they shall know,
Themselues, not women, are the cause of woe.
  Omnes. A Champion, a Champion. *Exeunt Omnes.*

[Scene. iii.]

Enter Atticus, Misogynos, *two Iudges, Notarie,*
Cryer, two Lawyers, and Attendants—And then
Lisandro, *and* Leonida *guarded.*

  Attic. That Equitie and Iustice both may meet,
In paralels, like to *Apollo's* Twinnes,
We haue ordayn'd this Session. In the which
Let all vnequall and impartiall thoughts
Be laid aside, with such regard of truth,
As not the name of Daughter, or the Bloud
Which we call ours, running in her veines, 10

---

123 before₍ₐ₎] G; ~,
141 baser] base
144 *Omnes.*] G; om.
  2 SD *two Lawyers,*] om.
  3 SD Leonida] Hortensia

May any way diuert vs. Therefore goe on,
And take your seat, stout Champion, and preuaile,
As is the truth you deale for, in this doubtfull,
And much ambiguous businesse.
   Misog.   So I wish.
               Passe to his seat with Trumpets.

      Enter to them Aurelia, *leading* Atlanta, Loretta,
           and two or three more women.

   Aurel. Braue Amazonian beautie, learned *Atlanta,*
Now is it time your intellectuall powers,
Of wit and iudgement shou'd aduance themselues   20
Against the forked tongues of Slanderers,
That pierce the spotlesse innocence of women,
And poyson sweetnesse with the breath of Malice.
So on, and take thy seat! It is our trust,
Th'euent will prosper, for our cause is iust.
   Atlan. That make me confident.   *Passe to the seat.*
   Attic.   Prepare the Court.
   Cryer. O yes! O yes! O yes! If there be any man
—or woman—in this Honourable Court—that can
produce—any lawfull cause—against either of the
Aduocates—why they should not bee admitted—
Let them now speake, or for euer hereafter hold
their peace—   30
   Attic. 'Tis well. Now sweare the Iudges.
   Notarie. Yee shall sweare by the sacred hand of
Atticus, not to respect the person of either of the
Offendors: but iustly and truly to waigh and ballance
the Reasons and Arguments of the deputed Aduocates,
and thereupon to determine and proceed in iudgement,
according to the Lawes of this Iland, as you tender the
pleasure of Royall *Atticus.*   40
   Both Iudges. To this we freely sweare.
   Attic. Now then, to your Arguments.
   Aurel. Atlanta, for poore innocent women.
   Attic. Misogynos for the men.

---

    15 wish.] G; wish—
    26 confident.] G; confident—

Atlan. It is an honour farre beyond my weaknesse,
(Most equall Iudges) that I am accepted,
I but a woman, before men to plead,
Dumbe feare and bashfulnesse to speake before
Bold Orators of State, men graue and wise,
That can at euery breathing pause, correct 50
The slipp'ry passages of a womans speech:
But yet withall my hopes are doubly arm'd.
  1. *Iudge.* How doubly arm'd?
  2. *Iudge.*   Presume not more then Reason.
  Atlan. First, that my bashfull weaknesse claymes excuse,
And is to speake before such temp'rate Iudges,
Who in their wisdome will, no doubt, conniue
At small defects in me a silly woman.
  1. *Lawyer.* Smoothly put on.
  2. *Lawyer.*   A quaint insinuation.
  Atlan. Next, that the cause I handle, is so iust,
And full of truth, as were corruption seated 60
Vpon your hearts (as who can euer doubt
Wisdome shou'd so decline) I wou'd not feare,
But that my pregnant Reasons soone shou'd purge,
And clense your secret bosomes from vntruth.
  1. *Lawyer.* A promising *Exordium.*
  2. *Lawyer.*   The successe is all.
  Atlan. I need not tell you what I come to prooue:
That rayling Woman-hater hath alreadie
With his foule breath belcht forth into the Ayre,
The shamelesse cause in question, and doth charge
The supple wax, the courteous-natur'd woman, 70
As blamefull for receiuing the impression
Of Iron-hearted man, in whom is grauen,
With curious and deceiuing Art, foule shapes
And stamps of much abhord impietie.
Wou'd any man, once hauing fixt his Seale
To any Deed, though after he repent
The Fact so done, rayle at the supple Wax,
As though that were the cause of his vndoing?

---

    70 courteous-natur'd] G2; courteous natur'd

O idle leuitie! Wax hath's vse,
And woman easly beares the mans abuse. 80
   1. *Lawyer.* Here's a by-blow.
   2. *Lawyer.* How can my Fencer ward it? Stay: he comes on.
   Misog. Hum. Doe you wax vpon me? as if man
Once hauing fixt the Seale of Armes of loue,
On waxen-harted woman, though another
Came after him, and did adulterate
The stampe imprinted on her, she, forsooth,
Must still be held excus'd. 'Tis weake, and fond,
And woman-like: you flye on waxen wings,
That melt against the Sunne. Therefore attend, 90
And I will proue vnto this honour'd Court,
In all their passions women are impetuous,
And beyond men, ten times more violent.
   Atlan. I grant you that. But who begins the motion,
And is first agent? for as I conceiue,
That's the cause in question.
   Misog. Deluding woman.
   Atlan.   Flattring and periur'd man.
   Misog. Did not th' inticing beautie of a woman,
Set Troy on fire?
   Atlan.   Did not man first begin
To tempt that beautie with the fire of lust? 100
   Misog. Beautie first tempts to lust.
   Atlan.   Lust tempteth Beautie:
Witnesse the vowes, the oaths, the protestations,
And Crocodile teares of base dissembling men,
To winne their shamelesse purpose: Whereof missing,
Then but obserue their Gifts, their Messages,
Their wanton Letters, and their amorous Sonnets,
Whereby they vent the smoke of their affections,
Readie to blind poore women, and put out
The Eye of Reason. But if still they faile,
Then come they on with vndermining cunning, 110
And with our Maides, our Pages and Attendants,
Corruptly worke and make insinuation,

---

   145 speech ₐ] ~,

Whilst they at hand with fained languishment,
Make shew as if they meant to dye for loue,
When they but swelter in the reeke of Lust.
But heere's not all: for if this all preuaile not,
Then they are vp againe, and with pale cheekes,
Like some poore Starueling, or some Mimick Ghost,
They stalke into the presence of their Mistris,
Fold vp their armes, hang downe their wanton heads,   120
Cast loue-sicke glances, and as wofull Commas,
In this dumbe Oratorie, now and then they breathe
A passionate sigh, whereat the gentle nature
Of milde compassionate woman once relenting,
Straight they fall out into such sweet complaints
Of their sad suffrings, tuning words of Art,
Able to melt a gentle Eye in teares,
As they doe speake. Then with officious dutie,
They licke a Moat off from her vpper garment,
Dust her curl'd Ruffe with their too busie fingers,   130
As if some dust were there: and many toyes
They vse to please, till side by side they ioyne,
And palme with palme supplies the amorous heart,
To pay a wanton kisse on Loues faire lips,
And then the Prize is wonne. Iudge therefore, Lords,
Whether the guilt doth lye on vs or them,
And as your Wisdomes find, saue or condemne.

    A Plaudite by the women, with shouts, crying, Atlanta,
                 Atlanta, Atlanta!

 Lisan. Truth hath she said in all.
 Leon.   O, but the Art   140
Of Woman—
  1. *Iudge.* Silence! you haue no voice in Court.
  2. *Iudge.* You haue your Aduocates, therefore must not speake.
  1. *Lawyer.* These Allegations are vnanswerable.
  2. *Lawyer.* The Court must needs allow them.
 Misog. Bragge not too fast! for all this glorious speech

---
    121 Commas] Comma's
    140 *Leon.*] *Hort.*
    140-141 Art/Of Woman—] Art of Woman—
    145 speech ₄] ~,

Is but a painted Pageant, made to vsher
Some homely Scauenger, and is borne vp,
Vpon the backes of Porters. It wants true worth,
To carrie State, and vsher learned Iudgement
Into this Court. For what a foolish reason, 150
Is it to say, Lust tempteth garish Beautie,
Because men court their wanton Mistresses,
In sundry formes of Complement! There's not
A Citie Tradesman throughout all the Streets,
From the East Chappell, to the Westerne Palace,
But knowes full well the garish setting out
Of Beautie in their shops will call in Customers
To cheapen ware: Beautie set forth to sale,
Wantons the bloud, and is mans tempting Stale.
    1. *Lawyer.* How boldly he comes on!
    2. *Lawyer.*   But marke his reasons. 160
    Misog. And this is woman, who well knowes her strength,
And trimmes her Beautie forth in blushing Pride,
To draw as doth the wanton Morning Sunne,
The eyes of men to gaze. But marke their natures,
And from their Cradles you shall see them take
Delight in making Babies, deuising Christnings,
Bidding of Gossips, calling to Vp-sittings,
And then to Festiuals, and solemne Churchings,
In imitation of the wanton ends
Their riper yeeres will ayme at. But goe further, 170
And looke vpon the very Mother of Mischiefe,
Who as her Daughters ripen, and doe bud
Their youthfull Spring, straight she instructs them how
To set a glosse on Beautie, adde a lustre
To the defects of Nature, how to vse
The mysterie of Painting, Curling, Powdring,
And with strange Periwigs, pin knots, Bordrings,
To deck them vp like to a Vintners Bush,
For men to gaze at on a Midsummer Night.

---

       153 Complement!] ~?
       157 shops_∧] ~?
       160 on!] ~?
       169 ends_∧] ~,

1. *Lawyer.* The tyde begins to turne.
2. *Lawyer.*   Women goe downe.   180
Misog. This done, they are instructed by like Art,
How to giue entertainment, and keepe distance
With all their Sutors, Friends, and Fauourites,
When to deny, and when to feed their hopes,
Now to draw on, and then againe put off,
To frowne and smile, to weepe and laugh out-right,
All in a breath, and all to trayne poore man
Into his ruine: Nay, by Art they know
How to forme all their gesture, how to adde
A *Venus* Mole on euery wanton cheeke,   190
To make a gracefull dimple when she laughes:
And (if her teeth be bad) to lispe and simper,
Thereby to hide that imperfection:
And these once learn'd, what wants the Tempter now,
To snare the stoutest Champion of men?
Therefore, graue Iudges, let me thus conclude:
Man tempts not woman, woman doth him delude.

A Plaudite by the Men with shouts, crying,
Misogynos, Misogynos, Misogynos!

1. *Lawyer.* Women, looke to't, the Fencer giues you a
veney.   200
2. *Lawyer.* Beleeue it, he hits home.
Misog.   Nay, I wou'd speake.
What Tyrannies, Oppressions, Massacres,
Women stand guiltie of: and which is more,
What Cities haue beene sackt and ruinate,
Kingdomes subuerted, Lands depopulated,
Monarchies ended! and all these by women.
Atlan. Base snarling Dogge, bite out thy slandrous tongue,
And spit it in the face of Innocence,
That at once all thy rancour may haue end:
And doe not still opprobriously condemne   210
Woman that bred thee, who in nothing more
Is guiltie of dishonour to her Sex

---
206 ended!] ~?
212 Sex₍ₐ₎] ~:

But that she hath brought forth so base a Viper,
To teare her reputation in his teeth,
As thou hast done.
    Misog.   O doe not scold, good woman!
    1. *Iudge.* Goe to the purpose.
    Atlan.   I forgot my selfe:
Therefore, graue Iudges, let this base Impostor
Tell me one man that euer gaue his life,
To keepe his vow safe and inuiolate,
Against the assaults of Lust: and for that one,   220
Ile find a thousand women, that to keepe
Their Chastities and Honours vndefil'd,
Haue laid their liues downe at base Tyrants feet.

        A Plaudit by Women, crying, Atlanta,
              Atlanta, Atlanta!

    1. *Lawyer.* This is but a flourish.
    2. *Lawyer.*   The Fencers Schoole-play beares it.
    Misog. What hath beene is not now: The Kalender
Of Women-Saints is fild vp long agoe:
For now a vniuersall leprosie,
Like to an Inundation, ouer-flowes,   230
And breakes vpon you all: scarce one is free
From wanton lightnesse and vaine leuitie.
    Atlan. None like to *Nero,* and *Heliogabulus.*
    Misog. Yes, wanton *Hellen* and *Cleopatra.*
    Atlan. I cou'd name more.
    Misog.   I, ten for one, of Women.
    Atlan. Sense-pleasing *Sardanapalus* is beyond
All Women that can be nam'd.
    Misog.   Ile name you one
Beyond all Men, th' insatiate *Messalina:*
Who when she had to satisfie her lust,
Imbrac'd the change of Louers, and was weakened   240
So farre, she could no longer hold it out:
And being askt if then she were satisfied,
She answered, No: for though she then were tyr'd,
No change could satisfie her appetite.

---

    243 answered] G; answerered

A Plaudite by the Men, crying, Misogynos,
Misogynos, Misogynos.

Atlan. O monstrous impietie!
Aurel. Stop the Detractors mouth: Away with him.
Women. Teare him in pieces.
Notarie.   Silence in the Court.
Attic. It is enough: My Lords, proceed to iudgement;   250
And lead away *Misogynos* to his Chamber.

The two Lawyers lead Misogynos *away.*

1. *Iudge.* Read the decree.
Notarie. We the sworne Iudges of this present Court,
In equall ballance hauing weigh'd the reasons,
And allegations of both Aduocates,
In their late Declamations, doe adiudge,
And here conclude that—
Attic.   Read out.
Notarie. That women are the first and worst temptations
To loue and lustfull folly: and to this   260
We are here present, ready to subscribe.
Atlan. You are impartiall, and we doe appeale
From you to Iudges more indifferent:
You are all men, and in this weightie businesse,
Graue Women should haue sate as Iudges with you.
Aurel. 'Tis true, 'tis true: Let vs haue iustice.
Attic. It is decreed already; attend the iudgement.
Aurel. Yet at the last let your *Aurelia* kneele,
And for the Offspring of your loynes and mine,
Begge fauour.
Attic. Peace.
Aurel.   You alwayes haue bin iust   270
In other causes; Will you in your owne
Be so vniust, seuere, nay tyrannous?
The very Beasts, by naturall instinct,
Preserue their issue; and will you be then,
More cruell and vnnaturall then they?
Attic. Arise; and know, A King is like a Starre,
By which each Subiect, as a Mariner,
Must steere his course. Iustice in Vs is ample,

From whom Inferiors will deriue example.
  Aurel. Oh, be not so obdurate!
  Attic.   I'le heare no more.   280
  Atlan. Yet, gracious Sir, for my indeuouring paines,
(Though fruitlesse now) let mee (a Stranger) beg
One boone—
  Attic. But not the freedome of *Leonida.*
  Atlan. Since she must die, I beg she may not basely
Be hurried forth amongst vnciuill men;
But that your Queene, and I, and some few others,
With any one of your attendant Lords,
May see her execution.
  Attic.   Take your desire.
  Leon. The blessed Heauens be thankfull to *Atlanta.*
  Lisan. And crowne her with all blessings.   290
  Attic. Take my thanks too. And now, my Lords, proceed,
And giue your finall censure.   *Exit* Atticus.

          Cornets, a flourish.

  Aurel.   Come, *Atlanta,* come;
Teares fill mine eyes, and Griefe doth strike me dumbe.

          Exit Aurelia, Atlanta, *and all the*
             Women, except Leonida.

  1. *Iudge. Leonida,* By the iudgement of this Court,
You are found guiltie as the Principall,
In the offence committed; for which, we doome you
(According to the Lawes of this our Iland)
To lose your Head.
  2. *Iudge.* And you withall, *Lisandro,*   300
By the like Law, must within fifteene daies,
Betake you to perpetuall banishment.
  Leon. Welcome, sweet death.
  Lisan.   Nothing can expiate
The Kings seuere Decree, and Her hard fate.   *Exeunt Omnes.*

---
    283 not the freedome] not the the freedome
    284 die,] ~;
    295 SD Aurelia, Atlanta] Italic in Q.
    295 SD *except* Leonida.] om.

Act. IIII. [Scene. i.]

Enter Iago *and* Sforza, *seuerall.*

Sforz. Health to your Honour.
Iago.   Noble *Sforza,* thankes.
Sforz. Have you not heard the newes?
Iago.   Of what, my Lord?
Sforz. Lisandro, and the Princesse.
Iago.   Not as yet.
Sforz. Then I'le resolue you.
Iago.   Pray you doe, my Lord.
Sforz. The Aduocates both vsed their vtmost skill,
To iustifie and quit the Sex they stood for,
With arguments, and reasons so profound
On eyther side, that it was hard to say,
Which way the scale of Iustice would incline.   10
  Iago. I ioy to heare it; And to say the truth,
Both Sexes equally should beare the blame;
For both offend alike. But pray' proceed.
  Sforz. At length, the Aduocate that stood for vs,
Preuail'd so farre, with his forc'd Oratorie,
The Lord *Nicanor* too, abetting him,
That maugre all the Amazonians wit,
Which was (indeed) beyond expression,
The sentence past against the female Sex;
And the poore Princesse is adiudg'd to death.   20
  Iago. The Heauens forbid! The Princesse doom'd to die?
  Sforz. Too true, my Lord: I heard the words pronounc'd.
  Iago. A sentence most vniust, and tyrannous.
Where's the Detractor?
  Sforz.   Crown'd with Victorie,
And intertain'd with Triumph.
  Iago.   That iust Heauen

Should suffer such an impious wretch to liue!
I must goe looke the Princesse; when must she dye?
   Sforz. Tomorrow's Sun beholds a daughters fall.
   Iago. A Sunne must rise tonight, to dimme that Sunne,
From the beholding such a horrid deed.   30
'Twas cruell in a King, for such a fact;
But in a Father, it is tyrannie.

Enter Misogynos.

   Sforz. Forbeare, my Lord, the times are dangerous.
See! here's the Champion.
   Iago. Looke how the Slaue glories in his conquest,
How insolent he stalkes!
Shall we indure such saucie impudence?   *Offers to draw.*
   Sforz. Put vp, put vp, my Lord,
He is not worth our indignation: 40
Let vs a-while obserue him for some sport.   *They withdraw.*

Enter Scanfardoe.

   Scanf. My noble Fencer, I congratulate
Your braue achieuements in the last dayes triumph.
   Misorg. I thanke you, Scholler. Was't not brauely done?
   Scanf. Done like thy selfe: the spirits of *Mantua*
And old *Diogenes* doubled in thee.
   Misog.   I thinke, I haue giuen
The Female reputation such a wound,
Will not be cured in haste.

Enter two Gentlemen.

   Iago. [*Aside.*] Ha, ha, ha, ha; Pernicious salue.   50
   1. *Gent.* Worthie *Misogynos.*
   2. *Gent.*   Noble Champion,
We doe applaud your merit, in the report
Of your late conquest.
   Misog.   Thanke you, Gentlemen;
Truth will preuaile, you see. I speake not for my selfe,

---

    28 Tomorrow's] To morrow's
    29 tonight] to night
    38 SD *Offers to draw.*] om.
    41 SD *They withdraw.*] om.
    44 achieuements] atchieuements
    52 applaud your] G2; applaud/Your
    54 see. I] G2; see./I

In my owne quarrel; but the generall good
Of all men in the world.
   1. *Gent.*   We know it, Sir.
   Iago. Degenerate Monster, how he iustifies
His slandrous forgeries!
   Misog.   But, Gentlemen,
How goes the rumour?
What do's the Multiude report of mee?   60
   1. *Gent.* Oh Sir, the Men applaud you infinitely;
But the Women—
   Misog.   I respect not them:
Their curses are my prayers.
   Iago.   Oh damn'd Rogue!
   1. *Gent.* If you'le be rul'd by me, go shew your selfe
Amongst them all in publique: O 'twill fret
Their very galls in pieces.
   Iago.   That was well.
Somebody second that, and we shall see
Excellent pastime; for they'le ne'r indure
His sight with any patience.
   Scanf.   Doe i'faith,
That they may see you haue conquer'd.   70
   Misog. And I will. But should they grow outragious—
   2. *Gent.* Feare not that: we'le all along with ye.
   Misog. Will you conduct me safe vnto my Schoole?
   Scanf. I, I, we'le be your Gard.   *Exeunt.*
   Sforz. Oh what a Coward 'tis!
   Iago.   You doe him wrong:
He fights not with his hands, but with his tongue.
Why doe I trifle time? I'le to the Court;
This crueltie afflicts my very soule.
Good my Lord, ioyne with me; we'le to the King,
And see if wee can alter this decree.   80

   54-55 selfe,/In] G2; selfe, in
   55 quarrel; but] G2; quarrel;/But
   55-56 good/Of] G2; good of
   58 forgeries!] ~?
   67 Somebody] Some body
   71 will. But] will./But
   75 'tis!] ~?

Oh 'tis a royal Princesse, faire, and chaste!
   Sforz. But her disdaine, my Lord, hath bin the cause
Of many hopefull Youths vntimely end;
'Tis that has harden'd both the Commons hearts,
And many a noble Peeres.
   Iago.   Why, what of that?
It is not fit affection should be forc'd:
Let's kneele vnto his Grace for her release.
Iustice (like Lightning) euer should appeare
To few mens ruine, but to all mens feare.   *Exeunt.*   90

Scene. ii.

Enter Nicanor, *and a Gentleman.*

   Nican. The Princesse suffers then?
   Gent.   This Morning, Sir,
Vnlesse the mercie of the King be found
More then is yet expected.
   Nican.   Oh my heart,
Canst thou indure to heare that heauie sound,
And wilt not burst with griefe?
   Gent.   Nay, good my Lord:
   Nican. Oh, worthie Sir, you did not know the ioyes
That we all lost in her. She was the hope,
And onely comfort of Sicilia;
And the last Branch was left of that faire stocke;
Which (if she dye) is wither'd, quite decay'd.   10
But I haue such a losse.
   Gent.   You haue indeed:
Yours is the greatest of a particular:
For you haue lost a beautious Spouse, my Lord;
And yet the rich hopes of a royall Crowne
Might mitigate your sorrow. You are next.
   Nican. Doe not renew my griefe with naming that.
Oh that it were tomorrow! happie day,
Bestow'd on some more meritorious,
That might continue long, for I am old.
I should be well content.

---
    3 heart] hearr
  17 tomorrow!] to morrow!

Gent.   Say not so: 20
There's no one merits that more then your selfe:
You are elected by the Kings owne house,
And generall consent of all the Realme,
For the Successour after his decease:
Whose life pray Heauen defend.
    Nican.   Amen, Amen,
And send him long to raigne; [*Aside.*] but not on earth.
Sir, you are neere the King; Pray, if you heare
His Highnesse aske for me, excuse me, Sir:
You see my sorrow's such, I am vnfit
To come into the presence of a King.   30
    Gent. I see it, Sir, and will report as much.   *Exit.*
    Nican. You will report a lye then; ha, ha, ha!
My Lungs will not afford me wind enough
To laugh my passions out. To gaine a Crowne,
Who would not at a funerall laugh and sing?
All men of wisedome would, and so will I:
Yet to the worlds eye, I am drown'd in teares,
And held most carefull of the King and State,
When I meane nothing lesse. *Lorenzo's* dead:
The scornefull Princesse, that refus'd my loue,   40
Is going to her death. The King, I know,
Cannot continue long: Then may I say,
As our Italian heires at fathers deaths,
Quid Iude, Reine ta soll.
The King alone made mee the King:
Me thinkes I feele the royall Diadem
Vpon my head already; ha, ha, ha!   *Exit.*

                  A dumbe shew.

    Enter two Mourners, Atlanta *with the Axe,* Leonida
all in white, her haire loose, hung with ribans; supported   50
on eyther side by two Ladies, Aurelia *following
as chiefe Mourner. Pase softly
ouer the stage.*

---

31 SD *Exit.*] G; om.
32 ha!] G; ~.
47 ha!] G; ~.

A Song in parts.
Whilst wee sing the dolefull knell
Of this Princesse passing-bell,
Let the Woods and Valleys ring
Ecchoes to our sorrowing;
And the Tenor of their Song,
Be ding, dong, ding, dong, dong, 60
  ding, dong, dong,
   ding, dong.
Nature now shall boast no more,
Of the riches of her Store,
Since in this her chiefest prize,
All the Stocke of beautie dies;
Then, what cruell heart can long
Forbeare to sing this sad ding dong?
  This sad ding dong,
   ding dong. 70
Fawnes and Siluans of the Woods,
Nimphes that haunt the Cristall flouds,
Sauage Beasts more milder then
The unrelenting hearts of men,
Be partakers of our mone,
And with vs sing ding dong, ding dong,
  ding dong, dong,
   ding dong.   *Exeunt Omnes.*

[Scene. iii.]

Enter Misogynos, *and* Swash.

Misog. Swash.
Swash. At your Buckler, Sir!
Misog. Perceiu'st thou nothing, *Swash?*
Swash.   How meane you, Sir?
Misog. No strange signe of alteration; hum.
Swash. Beyond imagination.
Misog.   How, good *Swash?*
Swash. Why, from a Fencer, you're turn'd Orator.
Misog. Oh! *Cedunt arma Togæ;* that's no wonder.

---
 2 Sir!] ~?

Perceiu'st thou nothing else? Looke I not pale?
Are not my armes infolded? my eyes fixt,
My head deiected, my words passionate,   10
And yet perceiu'st thou nothing?
    Swash.   Let me see.
Me thinkes, you looke Sir, like some desperate Gamester
That had lost all his estate in a dicing House:
You met not with those Money-changers, did you?
Or haue you falne amongst the female Sex,
And they haue paid you for your last dayes worke?
    Misog. No, no, thou art as wide, as short in my disease:
Thou neuer canst imagine what it is,
Vnlesse, I tell thee. *Swash,* I am in loue.
    Swash. Ha, ha, ha, in loue?   20
    Misog. Nay, 'tis such a wonder, *Swash,* I scarce beleeue,
It can be so, my selfe, and yet it is.
    Swash. The Deuill it is as soone, and sooner too:
You loue the Deuill, better then a woman.
    Misog. Oh, doe not say so, *Swash,* I doe recant.
    Swash. In loue? not possible:
This is some tempting Syren has bewitcht you.
    Misog. Oh! peace, good *Swash.*
    Swash. Some Cockatrice, the very Curse of man?
    Misog. No more, if thou dost loue me.
    Swash.   Your owne words.   30
I know not how to please you better, Sir.
Will you from Oratour, turne Heretike,
And sinne against your owne Conscience?
    Misog.   Oh, *Swash, Swash!*
Cupid, the little Fencer playd his Prize,
At seuerall weapons in *Atlanta's* eyes;
He challeng'd me, we met and both did try
His vtmost skill, to get the Victorie.

    11-12 see./Me] see, me
    12 some desperate] some/Desperate
    12-13 Gamester/That] Gamester, that
    13 estate in] estate/In
    13-14 House:/You] House: you
    14 not with] not/With
    35 eyes;] G; ~,

Lookes were oppos'd 'gainst lookes, and stead of swords,
Were banded frowne 'gainst frowne, and words 'gainst words.
But cunning *Cupid* forc't me to recoile: 40
For when he plaid at shrape, I had the foyle.
   Swash. Nay, now he is in loue, I see it plaine:
I was inspir'd with this Poeticall vaine,
When I fell first in loue: God bo'y yee, Sir:
I must goe looke another Master.
   Misog.   *Swash.*
   Swash. Y'are a dead man: beleeue it, Sir,
I would not giue two-pence for a Lease
Of a hundred pound a yeere made for your life.
Can you that haue bin at defiance with vm all,
Abused, arraigned vm, hang'd vm, if you could: 50
You hang'd vm more then halfe, you tooke away
All their good names, I'me sure; can you then hope,
That any will loue you? A Ladie, Sir,
Will sooner meet a Tinker in the street,
And try what Metall lyes within his Budget,
A Countesse lye with me, an Emperour
Take a poore Milke-maide, Sir, to be his Wife,
Before a Kitchen-Wench will fancie you.
   Misog. Doe not torment me, misbeleeuing Dolt,
I tell thee, I doe loue, and must enioy.   60
   Swash. Who, in the name of women, should this bee?
   Misog. What an obtuse Conception do'st thou beare?
Did not I tell thee, 'twas *Atlanta, Swash?*
   Swash. Who, the Amazonian Dame, your Aduocate,
A Masculine Feminine?
   Misog.   I, *Swash,*
She must be more then Female, has the power
To mollifie the temper of my Loue.
   Swash. Why, she's the greatest enemie you haue.
   Misog. The greater is my glorie, *Swash,* in that

---

    38 swords,] G; words,
    39 words.] ~ ˄
    40 forc't] forecast
    52 sure;] ~,
    64 the] G; she

Act IIII, Scene iiii 111

That hauing vanquisht all, I attaine her.   70
The Prize consists alone
In my eternall credit and renowne.
Oh, what a Race of wittie Oratours
Shall we beget betwixt vs: Come, good *Swash,*
Ile write a Letter to her presently,
Which thou shalt carry: if thou speedst, I sweare,
Thou shalt be *Swetnams* Heire.
   Swash.   The Deuill I feare,
Will dispossesse me of that Heritage.   *Exeunt.*

[Scene. iiii.]
Enter two Gentlemen.

   1. *Gent.* But are you sure she is beheaded, Sir?
   2. *Gent.* Most certaine, Sir, both by the Kings Decree,
And generall voyce of all, for instance see.
   1. *Gent.* The wofull'st sight that ere mine eyes beheld.
   2. *Gent.* A sight of griefe and horrour.
   1. *Gent.* It is a piece of the extremest Iustice
That euer Memory can Register.
   2. *Gent.* I, in a Father.
   1. *Gent.*   Oh, I pray forbeare,
The time is full of danger euery-where.   *Exeunt.* 10

[Scene. v.]
Enter Lisandro, *and the Guard.*

   Lisan. Good gentle friends, before I leaue the Land,
Suffer me to take my last fare-well
Of my owne dearest deare *Leonida.*
Accept this poore reward: would time permit
I would more largely recompence your loues.
   1. *Guard.* You haue preuail'd, my Lord, but pray bee briefe.
We are inioyn'd by strict Commission,
To see you shipt away this present tyde.
   Lisan. Indeed, I will.

---
   78 SD *Exeunt.*] om.
    5 sight that] sight,/That
    1 SD Lisandro] Lisander
    5 permit$_\wedge$] G; ~.

   1. *Guard.*   Then here you may behold,   10
All that it left of faire *Leonida.*   *Reveals her body.*
   Lisan. Oh—
   2. *Guard.*   How fare you, Sir.
   Lisan.   Oh, Gentlemen,
Can you behold this sacred Cabinet,
Which Nature once had made her Treasurie?
But now broke ope by sacrilegious hands,
And not let fall a teare: you are vnkind.
Not Marble but would wet at such a sight,
And cannot you? Oh strange stupiditie!
[*Addresses body.*] Thou meere Relike of my dearest Saint!
Vpon this Altar I will sacrifice   20
This Offering to appeaze thy murd'red Ghost.
   1. *Guard.* Restraine, my Lord, this Passion, we lament
As much as you, and grieue vnfaynedly
For her vntimely losse.
   Lisan. As much as I? Oh, 'tis not possible.
You temporize with sorrow: mine's sincere,
Which I will manifest to all the World.
See what a beauteous forme she yet retaynes,
In the despight of Fate, that men may see,
Death could not seize but on her mortall parts: 30
Her beautie was diuine and heauenly.
   1. *Guard.* Nay, good my Lord, dispatch, the time's but short.
   Lisan. Indeed, I will, to make an end of time:
For I can liue no longer, since that she,
For whose sake onely I held truce with time,
Hath left me desolate: no, diuinest loue,
What liuing was deny'd vs, weele enioy
In Immortalitie, where no Crueltie,
Vnder the forme of Iustice, dare appeare.
Sweet sacred Spirit, make not too much haste   40
To the Elizian Fields, stay but awhile,
And I will follow thee with swifter speed,
Then meditation: thus I seale my vow.   *Kisses her.*

---

   11 *Reveals her body.*] om.
   18 you? Oh] G; you,ˬ
   35 onely I] onely. I
   43 SD *her.*] om.

Me thinkes, I feele fresh heat, as if her soule
Had resum'd her former seate agen,
To solemnize this blessed Vnion,
In our last consummation, or else it stayes,
Awayting onely for my companie:
It does, indeed, and I haue done thee wrong,
To let thy heauenly eyes want me so long,   50
But now I come, deare Loue, Oh, oh!   *Stabs self.*
  1. *Guard.* What sound was that?
  2. *Guard.*   Oh, we are all vndone,
The Prince has slaine himselfe: what shall we doe?
  1. *Guard.* There is no way but one, let's leaue the Land:
If we stay heere, we shall be sure to dye,
And suffer for our too much lenitie,
Though we are innocent.
  2. *Guard.*   Then haste away:
The doome weele execute vpon our selues,
And ship with speed for Holland, there, no doubt,
We shall haue entertaynment;   60
There are warres threatned betwixt Spaine and them.
  1. *Guard.* Then let vs hoyse vp sayle, mercy receiue
Thy soule to Heauen, Earth to Earth we leaue.   *Exeunt.*

                    Enter Atlanta.

  Atlan. What spectacle is this? A man new slaine,
Close by the Princess Herse! Who is't? Oh, me,
The Noble Prince *Lisandro.* Cruell Fate,
Is there no hope of life? See, he looks vp,
Ile beare him out of the ayre, and stop his wound:
If there be any hope, I haue a Balme   70
Of knowne experience, in effecting cures
Almost impossible, and if the wound
Be not too deadly, will recouer him.   *Exit* Lorenzo.
              Enter Aurelia *and* Iago.
  Iago. Deare Queene, haue patience.
  Aurel.   How, *Iago,* patience?

---

51 SD *Stabs self.*] om.
60 entertaynment;] G; ~,
66 Princess] Princes
73 SD Lorenzo.] *Lorenzo.*

'Tis such a sinne, that were I guiltie of,
I should despayre of mercie. Can a Mother
Haue all the blessings both of Heauen and Earth,
The hopefull issue of a thousand soules
Extinct in one, and yet haue patience? 80
I wonder patient Heauen beares so long,
And not send thunder to destroy the Land.
The Earth, me thinkes, should vomit sulph'rous Damps,
To stifle and annoy both man and beast,
Seditious Hell should send blacke Furies forth,
To terrifie the hearts of tyrant Kings.
What say the people? doe they not exclaime,
And curse the seruile yoke, in which th'are bound
Vnder so mercilesse a Gouernour?

Iago. Madame, in euery mouth is heard to sound, 90
Nothing but murmurings and priuate whispers,
Tending to seuerall ends: but all conclude,
The King was too seuere for such a Fact.

Enter Atlanta.

Aurel. Atlanta, welcome. [*Looks upon body.*] Oh my child, my child,
There lies the summe of all my miserie!

Atlan. Gracious Madame, doe but heare me speake.

Aurel. Atlanta, I should wrong thy merit else.
What wouldst thou say?
Something I know, to mitigate my griefe. 100

Atlan. Rather to adde to your afflictions.
I am the Messenger of heauie Newes.
Lisandro, Prince of Naples—

Aurel. What of him?
Beholding the sad obiect of his loue,
His violent passion draue him to despayre,
And he hath slaine himselfe.

Iago. Disastrous chance!

Atlan. I found him gasping for his latest breath,

---

76 'Tis] G; Tis
95 welcome.] ~,
103 Naples—] ~,

And bore him to my Lord *Iago's* house,
I vs'd my best of skill to saue his life:
But all, I feare, in vaine: the mortall wound   110
I find incurable: yet I prolong'd
His life a little, that he yet drawes breath:
Goe you and visit him with vtmost speed:
The Queene and I will follow.
 Iago.   Goe? Ile runne. *Exit* Iago.
 Aurel. Was euer Father so vnmercifull?
But for that Monster that was cause of this,
That bloudie, cruell, and inhumane wretch,
That slanderous Detractor of our Sex,
That *Misogynos,* that blaphemous Slaue?
I will be so reueng'd.
     Enter Clowne.   120
 Atlan. Madame, no more, he is not worth your wrath:
Let me alone with him.
 Clown.   Whist, doe you heare?
 Atlan. How now, what art thou?
 Clown. Not your Seruant, and yet a Messenger,
No Seruingman, and yet an Vsher too.
 Atlan. What are you then, Sir? speake.
 Clown. That can resolue you, and yet cannot speake,
      Giues Lorenzo *letter.*
I am no Foole, I am a Fencer, Sir.
 Aurel. A Fencer, sirrah? ha, what Countrey-man?
 Clown. This Countrey-man, forsooth, but yet borne in
England.   130
 Aurel. How? borne in England, and this Countrey-man?
 Clown. I haue bin borne in many Countreyes, Madame,
But I thinke I am best be this Countrey-man,
For many take me for a silly one.
 Aurel. For a silly one?
 Clown.   I, a silly one.

---
 114 SD Iago.] *Iago.*
 115 vnmercifull?] G ~,
 118 Sex,] G; ~:
 121 more, he] more,/He
 127 *Giues* Lorenzo *letter.*] om.

Atlan. Oh, Madame, I haue such welcomenesse!
Aurel. For me, what is't?
Atlan. The baytes of women haue preuented vs,
And hee has intrapt himselfe.
Aurel. How, by what accident?
Atlan. Loue, Madam, loue, read that.
Aurel. How's this?

[*She reads.*]
"To the most wise and vertuous Amazon,   140
Chiefe pride and glorie of the Female Sex."
A promising induction: what's within?
"Magnanimous Ladie, maruell not,
That your once Aduersary do's submit himselfe
To your vnconquer'd beautie."
    Atlan. Cunning Slaue.
    Aurel. "Rather impute it to the power of loue,
Whose heauenly influence hath wrought in me,
So strange a Metamorphosis."
    Atlan. The very quintessence of flatterie.
    Aurel. "In so much, I vow hereafter, to spend all my dayes,   150
Deuoted to your seruice, it shall be
To expiate my former blasphemies:
My desire is shortly to visit you."
    Atlan. It shall be to your cost then.
    Aurel. "To make testimony of my hearty contrition,
Till when and euer I will protest my selfe,
To be the conuerted *Misogynist.*"
    Atlan. Ha, ha, ha, why, this is excellent!
Beyond imagination.
    Aurel. You must not slip this oportunitie.   160
    Atlan. Ile not let passe a minute: his owne man
Ile make an instrument to feed his follies
With a kind acceptance, and when he comes,
Let me alone to plot his punishment.

140-141 "To . . . Sex."] G; To . . . Sex.
143-145 "Magnanimous . . . beautie."] G; Magnanimous . . . beautie.
146-148 "Rather . . . Metamorphosis."] G; Rather . . . Metamorphosis.
150-153 "In . . . you."] G; In . . . you.
155-157 "To . . . *Misogynist.*"] G; to . . . *Misogynist.*
162 his follies/With] G; his/Follies with

Aurel. Excellent *Atlanta,* I applaud thy wit.

Atlan. Ile make him an example to all men,
That dares calumniate a womans fame.
Attend an answere, Ile reward thee well.

Clown. I thanke your Madame-ship, Ime glad o' this.
'Tis the best hit that euer Fencer gaue.   *Exeunt.* 170

---

170 'Tis] Tis

[Act. V. Scene. i.]

Enter Atticus, Iago, Sforza, *and* Nicanor.

Attic. How took the Girle her death? did she not raue?
Exclaime vpon me for the Iustice done
By a iust Father? how tooke Naples sonne
His Exile from our Land? What, no man speake?
My Lords, whence springs this alteration?
Why stand you thus amaz'd? Methinks your eyes
Are fixt in Meditation; and all here
Seeme like so many sencelesse Statues,
As if your soules had suffer'd an eclipse,
Betwixt your iudgements and affections: 10
Is it not so? 'Sdeath, no man answers?
Iago, you can tell: I'me sure you saw
The execution of *Leonida.*
Not yet a sillable? If once agen
We doe but aske the question, Death tyes vp
Your soules for euer. Call a Heads-man there.
If for our daughter this dumbe griefe proceed,
Why should not We lament as well as you?
I was her father; whose deare life I priz'd
Aboue mine owne, before she did transgresse: 20
And, could the Law haue so bin satisfi'd,
Mine should ha' paid the ransome of her cryme.
But, that the World should know our equitie,
Were she a thousand daughters she should die.
    Iago. I can forbeare no longer. Then (Sir) know,
It was about that time, when as the Sunne
Had newly climb'd ouer the Easterne hils,
To glad the world with his diurnall heat,
When the sad ministers of Iustice tooke
Your daughter from the bosome of the Queene   30

Whom now she had instructed to receiue
Deaths cold imbraces with alacritie:
Which she so well had learn'd, that shee did striue,
Like a too forward Scholler, to exceed
Her Teachers doctrine,
So cheerefully she went vnto the Block,
As if shee'd past vnto her nuptiall bed.
And as the trembling Bride when she espies
The Bridegroome hastily vnclothe himselfe,
And now beginning to approch the bed,   40
Then she began to quake and shrinke away,
To shun the separation of that head,
Which is imaginary onely, and not reall.
So, when she saw her Executioner
Stand readie to strike out that fatall blow,
Nature, her frailtie, and the alluring world,
Did then begin to oppose her constancie:
But she, whose mind was of a nobler frame,
Vanquish'd all oppositions, and imbrac'd
The stroke with courage beyond Womans strength;   50
And the last words she spoke, said, I reioyce
That I am free'd of Fathers tyrannie.

   Attic. Forbeare to vtter more. We are not pleas'd
With these vnpleasing accents: Leaue the world
So cheerefully, and speake of tyrannie:
She was not guiltie sure. We'le heare no more.

   Iago. Sir, but you shall: since you inforc'd me speake,
I will not leaue a sillable vntold.
You ask'd if Naples sonne were banish'd too?
Yes, he is banish'd euer from the sight   60
Of mortall eyes againe: for he is dead.

   Nican. Lisandro dead! By what occasion?

   Iago. I scorne to answer thee. The King shall know,
It was his chance vpon that haplesse houre,
To passe that way, conducted by his gard,
Towards his banishment; where he beheld
The wofull obiect of the Princesse head:
There might you see loue, pittie, rage, despaire,

Acting together in their seuerall shapes;
That it was hard to iudge, which of all those   70
Were most predominant. At last, despaire
Became sole Monarke of his passions,
Which drew him to this error: Hauing got
Leaue of his gard to celebrate his vowes,
Vnto that precious relique of his Saint,
Where hauing breath'd a mornfull Elegie,
After a thousand sighs, ten thousand grones,
Still crying out, *Leonida,* my loue!
Then, as his death were limited by hers,
He sacrifiz'd his life vnto her loue: 80
For there (vnluckily) he slew himselfe.   *The King withdraws.*
 Sforz. The King's displeas'd, my Lord.
 Iago. No matter: I'me glad I touch'd his conscience
To the quicke. Did you not see
How my relation chang'd his countenance,
As if my words ingendred in his brest
Some new-bred passions?
 Sforz.   Yes, and did obserue
How fearefully he gaz'd vpon vs all:
Pray heauen it proue not ominous.

                    Enter Queene.   90

 Iago. The Queene!
 Queen. Where is this King? this King? this tyrant? He
That would be cald The iust and righteous King,
When in his actions he is most vniust;
Beyond example, cruell, tyrannous?
Where is my daughter? Where's *Leonida?*
Where is *Lusippus* too, my first borne hope?
And where is deare *Lorenzo?* dead! all dead!
And would to God I were intomb'd with them,
Emptie of substance. Curse of Soueraigntie,   100
That feed'st thy fancie with deluding hopes
Of fickle shadowes; promising to one,
Eternitie of fame; and vnto all,

---

   81 *The King withdraws.*] om.
   98 dead! all dead!] dead? all dead?

To be accounted wise and vertuous,
Obseruing but your Lawes and iust decrees;
That vnder shew of being mercifull,
Art most vnkind, and cruell: nay, 'tis true. *The King withdraws.*
Goe where thou wilt, still will I follow thee,
And with my sad laments still beat thy eares,
Till all the world of thy iniustice heares. *Exeunt King and Queene.* 110
 Nican. This Physick works too strongly, and may proue
A deadly potion. *Sforza,* good my Lord,
If any anger be 'twixt you and I,
Let it lye buried now; and let's deuise
Some pastime to suppresse this heauinesse.
A melancholy King makes a sad Court.
 Iago. I neuer heard him speake so carefully
Of the Kings welfare. I, with all my heart.
 Sforz. Who'le vndertake this charge?
 Nican. I will, my Lord; Let the deuice be mine.   120
 Iago. I'le get the Amazon to ioyne with you:
Her rare inuention, and experience too,
In forraine Countries may auaile you much,
In some new quaint conceit.
 Nican.   Doe, good my Lord:
I'de ha't as soone presented as I could.
 Iago. Tonight, if it be possible: farewell.
I must goe looke her out.   *Exit* Iago *and* Sforza.
 Nican.   Ha, ha, ha, ha.
So by this meanes, I shall express my selfe
Studious and carefull.

---

107 SD *The King withdraws.*] om.
110 iniustice] iustice
111-112 proue/A] proue a
112-113 Lord,/If] Lord, if
113-114 I,/Let] I, let
114-115 deuise/Some] deuise/some
115-116 heauinesse./A] heauinesse. A
117 *Iago.*] G2; om.
125 as soone] assoone
126 Tonight,] To night,
127 *Exit* Iago *and* Sforza.] om.

Scene. ii.

Enter Atlanta *and* Avrelia.

Aurel. But dost thou thinke hee'le come?
Atlan. He cannot chuse.
I sent him such a louing answer backe
By his Solliciter, able to make
An Eunuch to come with the conceit.
The houre's almost at hand. Madam, command
A banquet be set forth: My charge shall be

Enter with a Banquet, Women.

To giue him intertainement: whilst your Grace,
Loretta, and the Ladies of your traine, 10
Or any others you shall please to appoint,
Be ready to surprise him. So 'tis well.
Now leaue the rest to mee.
    Aurel. My deare *Atlanta,* I commend thy care.
    Atlan. Call it my dutie, Madam, and the loue
I owe to sacred vertue, to defend
The fame of women. All withdraw awhile,
I thinke I heare him comming. I, 'tis he.   *Exeunt Women.*

Enter Misogynos *and* Swash.

    Swash. This is the place, Sir, she appoynted you. 20
    Misog. Is this the Orchard then,
Where I must pluck the fruit from that faire tree?
    Swash. [*Aside.*] I would it might proue Stone-fruit, and so choke
Him.
    Misog. Ha! what's here? a banquet?
    Swash. Banquet? Where?
    Misog. Readie prepar'd? why, this is excellent!
What a kind creature 'tis!
    Swash. Did not I say
How monstrously she lou'd you? Come, fall to.
    Misog. Before my Mistresse come?
    Swash. I'faith Sir, I;
This is but onely a prouocatiue,

---

19 SD Swash] *Swash*
23-24 Stone-fruit, and so choke/Him] Stone-fruit,/And so choke him
26 'tis!] ~?

To make you strong and lustie for the incounter. 30
   Misog. And here's Wine too;
Nothing but Bloud and Spirit. Fall to, *Swash.*
   Swash. A sweet thing is loue,
That fills both heart and mind:
There is no comfort in the world,
To women that are kind.
Here, Sir, I'le drinke to you.
   Misog. I would she would come away once: Now, methinks,
I could performe. And see! but wish and haue.

              Enter Atlanta. 40

   Atlan. Oh, are you come? I see you keep your houre.
   Misog. I should be sorry else.
   Atlan.   Nay, keepe your place.
   Misog. Will you sit downe then? [*To* Swash.] Sirrah!
Walke aloofe.
   Atlan. Let him be doing something. Here, take this.
                           Offers some food.
   Misog. I haue made bold to taste your Wine and Cates.
And when you please, we'le try the operation.
   Atlan. How?
   Misog. You know my mind.
   Atlan. You men are all so fickle, that poore we
Doe not know whom to trust.
But doe you loue me truely?
   Misog.   By this kisse. 50
   Atlan. No, saue that labour, Sir: I'le take your word.
Yet, how should I beleeue you, when so late
You rail'd against our Sex, and slander'd vs?
   Misog. Oh doe not thinke of that, that's done and gone.
Doe not recall what's past. I now recant:
And (by this hand) I loue thee truly, Loue.
   Atlan. May I beleeue all this?
   Misog.   Come hither, *Swash.*
How often haue I sworne to thee alone,

---

   32 Spirit. Fall] Spirit./Fall
   36-37 kind./Here,] G; kind. Here,
   43 Sirrah!] ~?   aloofe.] G; ~,
   45 SD *Offers some food.*] om.

I lou'd this Lady; neuer none but shee?
  Swash. Yes truely, that he has. 60
  Misog. You may be proud, I tell you, of my loue,
There is a thousand Women in this Towne,
To imbrace me, would clap their hands for ioy,
And run like so many wild Cats.
  Swash.   That they would,
I dare be sworne for vm,
And hang about him like so many Catch-poles,
He would ne'r get from vm,
And yet this happinesse is profer'd you.
  Atlan. Which I cannot refuse,
You haue, you know, such a preuayling tongue,
No woman can deny you any thing. 70
  Misog. Why, that was kindly spoke. Where shall wee meet?
  Atlan. Hearke in your eare, I'le tell you.
  Misog.   Best of all.
  Atlan. But—
  Misog. Doe you thinke me such a foole?
  Atlan. Till then farewell: I'le speedily returne.   *Exit* Atlanta.
  Misog. Why law now, *Swash,* I told thee she would yeeld,
No woman in the world can hold out long.
Oh beware when a man of Art courts a woman.
  Swash. I, or a Fencer, Sir: We lay vm flat before vs.
But, pray you tell me, Master, Doe you loue 80
This Lasse sincerely?
  Misog. Ha, ha, ha. Loue? that were a iest indeed,
To passe away the time for sport, or so;
Th'are made for nothing else:
And he that loues vm longer, is a foole.
  Swash. Me thinkes 'tis pittie to delude her, Sir:
I'faith she's a handsome wench.
  Misog.   Away, you Asse.
Delude? what are they good for else?
                  Enter Atlanta.
She comes againe. Out of the Orchard, Swash.   *Exit* Swash. 90
Welcome, Sweet heart.

---

    75 SD Atlanta.] *Atlanta.*
    90 SD *Exit* Swash.] om.

Atlan. Are you in priuate, Sir?
Misog. There's not an eye vnder the Horizon
That can behold vs; If Suspicion tell,
I'le beat her blind as euer Fencer was.
   Atlan. Sir, now you talke of Fencing, I heare you
Professe that noble Science.
   Misog. 'Tis most true.
   Atlan. I loue you, Sir, the better; 'tis a thing
I honour with my heart. If any one
Should scandalize or twit me with your loue,
You can defend my fame, and make such men—   100
   Misog. Creepe on their knees, aske thee forgiuenesse,
Or any other base submission.
   Atlan. Oh, what a happinesse shall I inioy!
But can you doe this if occasion serue?
   Misog. Would some were here to make experience,
That thou mightst see my skill.
   Atlan. Sir, that will I.   *Strike him.*
   Misog. How's this?
   Atlan. Impudent slaue,
How dar'st thou looke a Woman in the face,
Or commence loue to any: Specially to mee?   110
Thou know'st I'me vow'd thy publique enemie,
Which this, and this, and this shall testifie.
   Misog. Oh that I had a weapon, thou shouldst know,
A thousand women could not stand one blow,
From my vnconquerd arme.
   Atlan. That shall be tride.
I'le fit you, Sir, in your owne element.
I thinke thou darest not looke vpon a sword.
See there's a foyle: I will but thumpe you, Sir.
Thy life's reseru'd vnto a worse reuenge.   *Play.*
   Misog. Oh. Some Deuil's enterd in this Idol sure,   120
To make mee misbelieue. Oh.
   Atlan. Cowardly slaue. A Fencer? you? a Fidler.

---
   103 inioy!] ~?
   104 can] G; can can
   122 you?] G2; you ⸳

He cannot hold his weapon, gard his brest;
No, nor defend a thrust. Art not asham'd
Thus to disgrace that noble exercise?
   Misog. Oh: Hold, hold; I yeeld, I yeeld.
   Atlan. Has our Countrie meats fed you so high,
You needs must haue a stale for your base lust?
I'le satiate your sences ere I haue done:
And so much for your feeling: For your taste,   130
You haue had sufficient in your sweet-meats, Sir:
Your drinke too was perfum'd to please your smell.
   Misog. I, but I haue had but sowre sauce to vm.
   Atlan. Why then the Prouerbe holds. Now for your sight.
Madam, Come forth, and bring your followers.

        Enter all the Women.

   Misog. I'de rather see so many Cockatrices.
Oh that my eyes might be foreuer shut,
So that I might ne'r behold these Crocadils.
   Aurel. Where's this bawling Bandog?
   Omnes.   Here, here, here, here.   140
   Misog. Murder, murder, murder. I'me betraid.
I shall be torne in pieces. Murder, ho.
   Aurel. Is this the dogged Humorist that cals
Himselfe the woman-hater?
   Misog.   On my knees.
   Aurel. Dost thou reply, vile Monster? Binde him, come.
   Old Woman. Let me come to him, Ile so mumble him.
   Aurel. Remember faire *Leonida* my child,
Whose innocence was made a Sacrifice
To thy base Forgeries and Sophistrie.
   Omnes. Out, you abominable Rascall.   150
   Aurel. This for your hearing, Sir: now all is full.
   Misog. Ladies, Gentlewomen, sweet *Atlanta*, all,
Heare me but speake.
   Loret.   No, not a syllable.
You have spoke to match alreadie, you damn'd Rogue.

---

   123 weapon, gard] weapon,/Gard
   123-124 brest;/No,] brest; no,
   138 foreuer] for euer
   140 Bandog?/ G; ~.

But weele reward you for't. Skrew his iawes.
Misog.   Oh, oh, oh.
Aurel. Now, thou inhumane wretch, what punishment
Shall we inuent sufficient to inflict,
According to the height of our reuenge?
Omnes. Let's teare his limmes in pieces, ioynt from ioynt.
Misog. Oh, oh.   160
Scold. Three or foure paire of Pincers, now red hot,
Were excellent.
Loret.   Will not our Bodkings serue?
Aurel. Hang him, Slaue, shall he dye as noble a death
As *Cæsar* did? No, no: pinch him, pricke him.
Young Woman. I haue small Pins enow to serue vs all.
Scold. We cannot wish for better: take him vp,
And bind him to this Post.
Loret.   Faith, Post and Paire,
As good a Game as can be.
Aurel.   Come, let's to't,
Shuffle the Cards, and leaue out all the Knaues.
Atlan. No, the Knaues in at Post, and out at Paire.   170
Aurel. Shall it be so? Agreed! Deale round.
Scold.   First, stake.
Misog. Oh, oh, oh, oh.
Atlan. Passe.
Aurel. Passe.
Loret. Nay, Ile not passe it so.
Misog. Oh, oh.
Young Woman. Faith, Ile be in too.
Misog. Oh!

Enter two Old Women and Swash.

Aurel. Againe, for me too, I will vye it.   180
Misog. Oh.
Atlan. And for me, Ile not deny it.
Misog. Oh.
Loret. Ile see you, and revy't agen.

---

165 *Young Woman.*] *A Boy.*
171 Agreed! Deale] G; Agreed?/Deale
177 *Young Woman.*] *A Boy.*
179 Swash.] *Swash.*

Misog. Oh, oh.
Scold. For your two, Ile put in ten.
Misog. Oh, oh, oh, oh, oh.
Aurel. How now? stay, who's this?
Swash. I could not find the way out of the Orchard,
If I should ha' beene hang'd, but fell into these   190
Old Women's mouthes: but the best is, They had
No teeth to bite me, but my Grandame heere
Scratches most deuillishly.
  Atlan. Here's a Whelpe of the same Litter too.
Come hither Sirrah, doe you know this man?
  Swash. Yes, forsooth, I know him,
He was my Master once, want of a better.
  Loret. Then you were one of his Confederates, Sir.
  Swash. I his Confederate? I defye him,
He knowes I always gaue him good counsell,   200
If he had had the grace to follow it:
Here he is himselfe, let him deny't if he can.
  Misog. Oh, oh, oh!
  Swash. Did not I euer say, Master, take heed,
Wrong not kind Gentlewomen,
Honest louing women? Many a time
Haue I beene beaten by him blacke and blue,
For looking on a woman; is't not true?
  Misog. Oh, oh.
  Swash.   You see his bringing vp,
To make a mouth at all this companie.   210
  Aurel. This is an honest fellow; he shall escape.
Sirrah, thou lou'st a woman?
  Swash. I, with all my heart.
  Scold.   He lookes as if he did.
  Atlan. Well, stand aside, weele imploy you anon:
Forbeare your tortors yet, something is hid,
That we must haue reueal'd, and he himselfe
Shall be his owne accuser: you all know,

---

191 Women's] Women s
191-192 is, They had/No] is,/They had no
203 oh!] G; oh,
208 woman;] G; ~,
213 Scold.] ~,

He hath arraign'd vs for inconstancie:
But now weele arraigne him, and iudge him too,
This is womans counsell: Madame, we make you   220
Ladie Chiefe Iustice of this Female Court,
Mistris Recorder, I. *Loretta,* you,
Sit for the Notarie: Crier, she:
The rest shall beare inferior Offices,
As Keepers, Seriants, Executioners.
   Swash. Ide rather be a Hangman then a Seriant:
Yet there's no great difference, if one will not,
T'other must.
   Atlan.   Mother, goe you and call a Iurie full,
Of which y'are the fore-woman.
   1. *Old Woman.* Thanke you forsooth, Ile fetch one presently: 230
'Tis fit he should be scratcht, and please your Grace:
Sure, he is no man.
   Atlan. We want a Barre. O, these two foyles shall serue:
One stucke i' the Earth, and crosse it from this Tree.
Now take your places, bring him to the Barre,
Sirrah, vngag him.
   Swash.   Let him be gag'd still:
Then you are sure what e'r you say to him,
He cannot contradict you.
   Atlan.   Pull it out.
   Swash. Doe not bite y'are best.
   Misog. Oh, that I were a Serpent for your sakes,   240
Bearing a thousand stings.
   Aurel.   Worse then thou art,
Thou canst not wish to be, abortiue wretch.
Bring him to the Barre.
   Swash. You'ld not be rul'd by me: I told you o'this,
And now you see what followes. Hanging's the least,
What-eu'r followes that.
   Aurel.   Clarke of the Peace,
Reade the Indictment.

---

     223 Crier,] *Crier,*
     240 Oh,] ~.
     245 followes. Hanging's] followes,/Hanging's
     245-246 least,/What-eu'r] least, what-eu'r

    Scold.   Silence in the Court.
    Swash. [*Aside.*] Silence? and none but women? That were strange!
    Loret. Misogynos, hold vp thy hand.
    Swash. His name is *Swetnam,* not *Misogynos.*   250
That's but a borrowed name.
    Misog.   Peace, you Rogue,
Will you discouer me?
    Aurel.   *Swetnam* is his name.
    Swash. I, *Ioseph Swetnam,* that's his name, forsooth,
Ioseph the Iew was a better Gentile farre.
    Loret. Then *Ioseph Swetnam, alias Misogynos,
Alias Molastomus, alias* the *Woman-hater.*
    Swash. How came he by all these names?
I haue heard many say, he was neu'r christen'd.
    Loret. Thou are here indicted by these names, that thou,
Contrary to nature, and the peace of this Land,   260
Hast wickedly and maliciously slandred,
Maligned, and opprobriously defamed the ciuill societie
Of the whole Sex of women: therefore speake,
Guiltie, or not guiltie?
    Misog.   Not guiltie.
    Swash.   Hum.
    Omnes. Not guiltie?
    Misog.   No, not guiltie.
    Aurel. Darest thou denie a truth so manifest?
Didst thou not lately both by word, and deed,
Publish a Pamphlet in disgrace of vs,
And of all women-kind?
    Misog.   No, no, no, not I.
    Swash. Hum.   270
    Atlan. Calling vs tyrannous, ambitious, cruell?
    Aurel. Comparing vs to Serpents, Crocodiles
For Dissimulation, *Hienas* for Subtilties,
Such like?
    Loret. And farre worse:

---

    265 guiltie?] ~.
    273 *Hienas*] *Hiena's*

That we are all the Deuils agents, to seduce Man agen?
  Scold. That all our studies are but to delude
Our credulous Husbands?
  Misog.   I denie all this.
  Swash. Hum.
  Loret. Nay more, Thou dost affirme, without distinction,
All married Wiues are the Deuils Hackneyes,   280
To carrie their Husbands to Hell.
  Aurel. Inhumane Monster, hast thou neu'r a Mother?
  Swash. No, forsooth, he is a *Succubus,* begot
Betwixt a Deuill and a Witch.
  Misog. If I did any such, let it be produc'd.
  Atlan. Bring in the Books for a firme Euidence,
And bid the Iurie giue the Verdict vp.

Enter two Old Women.

  Old Women. Guiltie, guiltie, guiltie.
Guiltie of Woman-slander, and defamation.   290
  Atlan. Produce the Bookes, and reade the Title of vm.
  *Loret. The Arraignment of idle, froward, and vnconstant
women.*
  Aurel. What say you, Sir, to this?
  Misog. Shew me my name, and then Ile yeeld vnto't.
  Aurel. No, that's your policie and cowardise,
You durst not publish, what you dar'd to write,
Thy man is witnesse to't: [*To* Swash.] sirrah, confesse,
Or you shall eu'n be seru'd of the same sawce.
  Swash. No, no, no, no, Ile tell you all,
He is no Fencer, that's but for a shew,   300
For feare of being beaten: the best Clarke,
For cowardise that can be in the World,
To terrifie the Female Champions,
He was in England, a poore Scholer first,
And came to Medley, to eate Cakes and Creame,
At my old Mothers house; she trusted him,

---

  275 agents, to] G; agents,/To
  279 more, Thou] more,/Thou
  292 *froward, and*] *froward,/And*
  292-293 *The . . . women.*] Roman in Q
  306 house;] ~,   him,] ~:

At least some sixteene shillings o' the score,
And he perswaded her, he would make me
A Scholer of the Vniuersitie,
Which she, kind Foole, beleeu'd: He neu'r taught me   310
Any Lesson, but to raile against women,
That was my morning and my euening Lecture.
And in one yeere he runne away from thence,
And then he tooke the habit of a Fencer:
And set vp Schoole at Bristow: there he liu'd
A yeere or two, till he had writ this Booke:
And then the women beat him out the Towne,
And then we came to London: there forsooth,
He put his Booke i' the Presse, and publisht it,
And made a thousand men and wiues fall out.   320
Till two or three good wenches, in meere spight,
Laid their heads together, and rail'd him out of th'Land,
Then we came hither: this is all forsooth.
  Aurel. 'Tis eu'n enough.
  Misog. 'Tis all as false as women.
  Omnes.   Stop his mouth.
  Atlan. Either be quiet, or y'are gag'd agen.
  Aurel. Proceed in Iudgement.
  Atlan.   Madame, thus it is.
First, he shall weare this Mouzell, to expresse
His barking humour against women-kind.
And he shall be led, and publike showne,   330
In euery Street i'the Citie, and be bound
In certaine places to a Post or Stake,
And bayted by all the honest women in the Parish.
  Misog. Is that the worst? there will not one be found
In all the Citie.
  Omnes.   Out, you lying Rascall.
Forbeare a little.
  Atlan. Then he shal be whipt quite thorow the Land,
Till he come to the Sea-Coast, and then be shipt,
And sent to liue amongst the Infidels.

---

309 Vniuersitie,] Niniuersitie,
309-310 Vniuersitie,/Which] G2; Niniuersitie, which
310-311 me/Any] G2; me any

Omnes. Oh, the Lord preserue your Grace.
Loret. Oh, oh, oh. 340
  Aurel. Call in his Bookes,
And let vm all be burn'd and cast away,
And his Arraignment now put i' the Presse,
That he may liue a shame vnto his Sex.
  Atlan. Sirrah, the charge be yours: which if you faile,
You shall be vs'd so too: if well perform'd,
You shall be well rewarded. Breake vp Court.
  Omnes. Away, you bawling Mastiffe.
  Clown. Pish, pish.   *Exeunt Omnes.*

[Scene. iii.]

Enter Atticus, Sforza, Nicanor, *and one or
two Lords more.*

  Attic. Why doe you thus pursue me? Can no place
Shelter a King from being bayted thus
With Acclamations beyond sufferance
Of Maiestie, or mortall strength to beare?
We will indure't no longer. Where's our Guard?
Where is *Aurelia?* where's *Iago* gone?
To studie new Inuectiues? If agen
They dare but vtter the least syllable, 10
Or smallest title of inueteracie,
They shall not breathe a minute. Must a Prince
Be checkt, and schooled, pursued and scolded at,
For executing Iustice?
  Nican.   Royall, Sir.
Be pleased, to cast away these Discontents.
Iago's sorrie for his bold offence.
The Queene repents her too, and all the Court
Is clowded o'r with griefe: your sadnesse, Sir,
Fils euery Subiects heart with heauinesse.
Will't please your Highnesse to behold some pastime? 20
There is a Maske and other sports prepar'd:
Prepared to solace you,

---

3 *Attic.*] *King.* All *King* headings in this scene are normalized to *Attic.*
20 pastime?] G; ~,

To steale away your sorrowes.
 Attic.   Who's that spoke?
Nicanor, is't hee? I thought as much:
I knew no other would be halfe so kind,
Nor carefull of our health: doe what thou wilt,
We will deny nothing that thou demandest,
My dearest Comforter, stay to my age,
The hope of Sicilie lyes now in thee.
Come sit by vs, weele see what new deuice   30
Thy diligence—
 Nican. My dutie.
 Attic.   No, thy loue
Hath studied to delight thy Soueraigne.
Come sit, *Nicanor.*
 Nican. Pardon, Sir, awhile,
Ile giue command to see it straight perform'd,
And instantly returne.
 Attic.   Make no delay:
We haue no ioy but in thy companie.
 Nican. [*Aside.*] Nor I no Hell, but thy continuance.
Ile present that will shorten it, I hope.   *Exit.*
 Attic. Sforza, thou louest me too: come neerer vs:
But old *Iago* is a froward Lord,   40
Honest, but lenatiue, ore-swaid too much
With pittie against Iustice, that's not good:
Indeed it is not in a Counsellor.
And he has too much of woman, otherwise
He might be Ruler of a Monarchie,
For policie and wisdome. *Sforza* sit,
Take you your places to behold this Maske.

      Enter Nicanor.

 Nican. Now they are readie.
 Attic.   Let vm enter then.
Come sit by vs, *Nicanor,* and describe   50
The meaning, as they enter.
     Enter Iago, *and the Queene.*

---

 38 SD *Exit.*] om.
 42 pittie] G; pitt e

Iago.   Heere your Grace
May vndiscouered sit, and view the Maske,
And see how 'tis affected by the King:
I know, 'twill nip him to the verie soule.

                Enter Musicke, dance.
The Maskers.
  Nican. He that leads the Dance,
Is called wilfull Ignorance.
  Sforz. The next that pryes on euery side,   60
As if feare his feet did guide,
Is held a wretch of base condition,
He is titled false Suspition.
  Nican. The third is of a bolder Faction,
But more deadly, 'tis Detraction.
The last is Crueltie, a King that long,
In seeming good, did sacred Iustice wrong.
  Attic. This Moral's meant by me: by heauen it is,
By Heauen, indeed: for nothing else had power
To make me see my Follies. I confesse,   70
'Twas wilfull Ignorance, and Selfe-conceit,
Sooth'd with Hypocrisie, that drew me first
Into suspition of my Daughters loue,
And call'd it Disobedience: false Suspect,
'Twas thou possest me, that *Leonida*
Was spotted and vnchaste.
  Nican. [*Aside.*]   So, now it workes.
  Attic. And then Detraction prou'd a deadly Foe.
  Iago. I knew 'twould take effect.
  Aurel.   Most happily.
  Attic. I am that King did sacred Iustice wrong,
Vnder a shew of Iustice; now 'tis plaine,   80
It was my crueltie, not her desert,
That sacrific'd my Child to pallid Death.
Lisandro slew himselfe, but I, not he
Must answere for that guiltlesse bloud was spilt:
For I was Authour on't, my Crueltie,

---
    60 *Sforz.*] *King.*
    80 Iustice;] G; ~,

Diuorcing two such Louers, was the cause
That drew him to despayre. How they all gaze,
Whisper together, and then point at me,
As if they here had being! yes they haue:
But it shall proue a restlesse bed for them.   90
Why doe they not begin?

Enter Repentance.

  Nican. Belike they want some of their companie.
  Attic. But stay, who's that descends so prosperously,
With such sweet sounding Musike? All obserue.

Musike, dance.

See how the splendor of that Maiestie,
That came from Heauen, hath disperst away
Suspition, Ignorance, and Crueltie,
And instantly o'rcome Detraction too,   100
Those enemies to vertue, foes to man,
Are vanisht from my sight, and from my heart.
But let Repentance stay. Ha, shallow Foole,
Doe I so slightly bid her? On my knees,
She must be followed, call'd and su'd vnto,
And by continuall Prayers, woo'd, and wonne,
Which I will neuer cease, if not too late.
I doe repent me, let this Sacrifice
Make satisfaction for those fore-past Crimes
My ignorant soule committed.
  Repen.   'Tis accepted.   110
Imbrace me freely, rise: neuer too late
To call vpon Repentance.
  Nican.   [*Aside.*] I am trapt.
Oh, the great Deuill! whose deuice was this?
Now all will be reueal'd. I neuer dream't
Vpon Repentance, I: but now I see,
Truth will discouer all mens Trecherie.
  Attic. Liue euer in my bosome. What meanes this?

---

    97 ˄ See] *Nic.* See
    105 vnto,] vuto,

Enter Lorenzo, *as an old Shepherd,* Lisandro,
      Leonida, *as a Siluan Nymph.*

 Loren. If a Siluan's rude behauior   120
May not heere despaire of fauour:
Then to thee this newes I bring,
Thou art call'd the righteous King,
And as Fame do's make report,
Heere liues Iustice in thy Court:
Know, that all the Happinesse
I did in this World possesse,
Was my onely Daughter, who
Pan did on my age bestow;
She was named *Claribell,*   130
Whom *Palemon* loued well:
And she lou'd him as well againe;
So that nothing did remaine,
But the tying *Hymens* Knot.
But it chanced so, God wot,
That an old decrepit man
Most prepostrously began,
With flatt'ring words to woo my Daughter,
But being still deny'd, he after
Turn'd his loue to mortall hate   140
Claribell to ruinate,
Striuing to o'rpresse her fame,
With Lust, Contempt, Reproch, and Shame.
 Attic. What wouldst thou haue Vs doe? Good Father, speake.
 Loren. This fellow hath subborn'd a rout
Of some base Villaines here-about,
To take away my daughters life,
Or else to rauish her. To end this strife
Be pleas'd to ioyne these Louers hands
Into sacred nuptiall bands.   150

---
  118 SD *as an old Shepherd,*] om.
  119 SD *as a Siluan*] *a Siluan*
  129 bestow;] G; ~,
  143 Contempt,] G;
  144 doe? Good] doe?/Good

Sforz. Nothing but put vm both together, Sir.
The good old Shepheard would faine ha't a match.
    Attic. We are content. Come giue Vs both your hands.
    Loren. You are a King; yet they are loth
To take your word without an othe.
    Attic. As We are King of Sicil, 'tis confirm'd
Firme, to be reuoked neuer,
Vntill death their liues disseuer.
    Loren. Princes, discouer: Here are witnesses
Inow to testifie this royall match   160
              [Lisandro *and* Leonida *throw off disguises.*]
    Attic. My daughter, and *Lisandro,* liuing?
    Loren. Nay, wonder not, my Liege, your oath is past.
    Attic. Which thus, and thus, and thus I ratifie:
There is but one step more, and farewell all.
    Aurel. Oh, I am made immortall with this sight:
My daughter, and *Lisandro,* both aliue?
    Iago. This is no newes to mee: yet teares of ioy
Ore-flowes mine eyes to see this vnitie.
    Attic. Oh daughter, I haue done thee too much wrong: 170
And, noble Prince, We now confesse Our errour:
But heauen be prais'd that you haue both escap'd
The tyrannie of Our vniust decree.
    Aurel. What happie accident preseru'd your liues?
Whose was the proiect? Was it thine, old man?
    Loren. Madam, 'twas mine: [*Throws off Siluan disguise.*]
              Those that I could not saue
By eloquence, by policie I haue.
    Attic. Worthie *Atlanta,* thou hast merited
Beyond all imitation. We are made
Too poore to gratifie thy high deserts.   180
    Loren. Dread Soueraigne,
All my deserts, my selfe, and what I haue,
Thus I throw downe before your Highnesse feet.
              [*Throws off Amazon disguise.*]
    Attic. My Sonne *Lorenzo!* Oh, assist, my Lords.
The current of my ioy's so violent,

---

    161 Lisandro . . . *disguises.*] om.

It does o'r-come my spirits. Worthy Sonne,
Welcome from death, from bands, captiuitie.
   Aurel. Welcome into my bosome as my soule.
   Leon. My princely Brother, could I adde a loue   190
Vnto that dutie that I owe for life,
I am ingag'd vnto't, you are my lifes Protector,
And my Brother.
   Lisan. And for a life I stand indebted too,
Which Ile detayne, onely to honour you.
   Omnes. And on our knees we must this dutie tender,
To you our Patron, and our Fames Defender.
   Repen. Behold the ioyes Repentance brings with her,
Thy blessings are made full in Heauen and Earth.
   Attic. Was euer Father happier in a Sonne,   200
Or euer Kingdome had more hopefull Prince?
But in a loyall Subiect, neuer King
More blest then we are: and the grace we owe,
Though farre too poore to quittance, shall make known,
Thy loue and merit. Now we can discerne
Our friends from flatt'rers. *Nicanor,* as for you,
But that this houre is sacred vnto ioy,
Thy life should pay the ransome of thy guilt.
   Nican. Your Graces pardon. 'Twas not pride of state,
But her disdaine, the first inspir'd in me   210
This hope of Soueraigntie.
   Attic.   Well, we forgiue.
Learne to liue honest now. Come, beautyous Queene,
We hope that all are pleas'd: and now you see,
In vaine we striue to crosse, what Heauens decree.

FINIS

---

190 *Leon.*] *Prince.*

EPILOGVE

Enter Swetnam *muzzled, hal'd in by Women.*
Swetnam. *Why doe you hale me thus? Is't not enough,*
I haue withstood a tryall? beene arraign'd?
Indured the torture of sharp-pointed Needles?
The Whip? and old Wiues Nayles? but I must stand,
To haue another Iurie passe on me?
    Loret. *It was a generall wrong; therefore must haue*
A generall tryall, and a Iudgement too.
    Leon. *The greatest wrong was mine; he sought my life:*
Which fact I freely pardon to approoue   10
Women are neither tyrannous, nor cruell,
Though you report vs so.
    Swetnam.   *I now repent,*
And thus to you (kind Iudges) I appeale.
Me thinkes, I see no anger in your eyes:
Mercie and Beautie best doe sympathize:
And here for-euer I put off this shape,
And with it all my spleene and malice too,
And vow to let no time or act escape,
In which my seruice may be shewne to you.
And this my hand, which did my shame commence,   20
Shall with my Sword be vs'd in your defence.

FINIS

Table of Grosart's Emendations

Following is a table of the emendations suggested by Alexander B. Grosart in his edition. The lemma in every case is from the present edition. G2 designates changes suggested by Grosart in his introductory notes, suggestions that he said "re-readings . . . yielded," which were compiled after his edition was printed. I have not noted typographical errors in his text which he later corrected in his introduction. Not included are those emendations which I have adopted for the present edition; note of those is made at the foot of the appropriate page of the text. Except where it was unavoidable, I have deleted Grosart's square brackets; he was inconsistent with their usage, and note of them here will not aid understanding. Where, for instance, he wrote "giue [him] his," I have represented his suggestion as "giue him his."

Prologue

6 dayes] daye's
13 slanders$_\wedge$] ~,

Act I, Scene i

  4 Prince,] ~ $_\wedge$
  7 Foe.] ~ $_\wedge$
 17 fear'd,$_\wedge$] ~ —
 28 "Death . . . sorrow."] "Death . . . sorrow":
 31 end: for] end;/For
 40 3. *Lord.*] 3. *Lord,* Sforza
 70 liuing, as] liuing,—as
 77 him.$_\wedge$] ~ *Exit Nic.*
 92 cause;$_\wedge$] ~ *Exit Nicanor.*
116 dead—] dead,—
145 forsake thy] G; forsake/Thy G2
146 Libertie? and] G; Libertie/And G2
147 Captiuitie, or] G; Captiuitie,/Or G2
148 both? Yet,] G; both?/Yet, G2
172 Boy,] ~ :
178 giue his] giue him his

I, ii

10 Puffe,] Puff-e,
11 I am] I'm
19 ifaith;] ~:
26 haue.] ~;
57 Fencing Boy;] "Fencing, Boy";
58 *Swash;*] *Swash:*
61 Nose.] ~?
65 Lord.] ~:
87-88 you now./Ile] you;/Now Ile
92 Duellist,] ~ ∧
95 publike, I am] publike; I'm
115 wicked.∧] wicked, Dissemblers.
117 Dissemblers, the very]∧ The very
157 hundreth] G2; hundredth
159 doubt,] ~ ∧
177 that,] ~ ∧

I, iii

2 yet.] ~;
3 to obserue] t'obserue
7 the offences] th'offences
15 grace,] ~;
16 Vertue,] ~;
18 Seat,] ~;
20 Clemencie,] ~;   inthron'd.] ~:
23 alone,] ~ ∧
33 sonnes,] ~;
39 Nature,] ~;
40 Euen] E'en
41 wonder∧] ~,   amazement,] ~;
43 *Leonida,*] ~;
47 Princes,] ~;
52 'Twas] Twas   be awhile] be/Awhile
52-53 restraind,/For] restraind; for
54 Guardian,] ~;
55 'tis] it is
67 proue] ~;   ly'st] lyest
68 thou hast] th' hast
70 wrong.] ~:
82 Lepanto,] ~;
83 vent'rous,] venturous,
85-86 hand/Defac'd] hand defac'd
86 the Impression] Th' Impression
86-87 Effigies/In] Effigies in
87 your memories] Your mem'ries
97 louest] lou'st
101 yet,] ~;

103 To obserue] T'obserue
105 discontent,] ~;
111-112 consent,/And] consent, and
115 Diadem,] ~;

II, i

7 losing you,] ~;
11-12 her/In whom my] her in whom/My
14 instinct,] ~ ∧
17 desist,] ~;
49 SD *She hesitates.*] *Seems to decline it.*
84 ith'] i'th
90 againe,] ~;
98 charg'd] charged
128 ∧Your] Did Your
143 know'st] knowst
170 habit,] ~;

II, ii

5 truly,] ~.
8 *Loretta.* Troth,] *Loretta,* troth,
21 takest] tak'st
23 You haue] G2; you've
42 report,] ~;
43 agen,] ~:
48 Mistris,] ~;
57 Father,] ~ ∧
63 minde,] ~;
75 wisdomes] wisdome's
78 Charitie,] ~.
90 aduentrous,] ~!
98 liue,] ~;
100 and protesting,] and your protesting,
102 publike.] ~;
106 too,] ~;
115 enough!] ~.
120 ha, ha!] ~ ha!
122 must not.] must not trust me.
139 vs,] ~;
140 followed,] ~;
150 well. Where] well; where
155 discouerie∧] ~,
157 I am] I'm

II, iii

7 yours] your's
12 in ioying] inioying
19 infection,] ~;

III, i

11 Daughter] daughter   hope$_\wedge$] ~.
12 Sicilie] G; Sicilia G2
17 easly] easily
27 Reuenge,] ~;
64 Fort's] Fort is
89 Kings] King's
92 deuice;] ~:
124 seeke,] ~ $_\wedge$
135 discouer it.] discouer't.

III, ii

44 opinion: They] opinion: that They
57 Women,] ~;
64 I'me] I am
72 Attomes] Attome's
136 contempt,] ~;
140 base] G2; basest
141 baser] base G; basest G2

III, iii

10 ours, running] ours, now running
15 SD *Passe*] *Passes*
26 SD *Passe*] *Passes*
42 then,] ~ $_\wedge$
49 State,] ~;
63 purge,] ~ $_\wedge$
79 hath's] hath his
101 Beautie:] ~.
142 Aduocates,] aduocates,
183 Fauourites,] ~;
185 off,] ~;
194 now,] ~ $_\wedge$
241 out:] ~.
250 iudgement;] ~:
256 Aduocates,] ~ $_\wedge$
257 adiudge,] ~.
274 then,] ~ $_\wedge$
284 die,] ~:
287 Lords,] ~ $_\wedge$

IV, i

7 for,] ~;
13 pray'] G2; pray
28 daughters] daughter's
44 dayes] daye's
46 *Mantua*] *Mantuan*
50 slaue.] ~!
51 Misogynos.] ~!

51-52 Champion,/We] G2; Champion, we
52 applaud your] G2; applaud/Your
53-54 Gentlemen;/Truth] G2; Gentlemen; truth
58-59 Gentlemen,/How] Gentlemen, how
62-63 them:/Their] them: their
69-70 i'faith,/That] i'faith, that
83 Youths] Youths'

IV, ii

17 happie day,] ~,—
18 some] G2; someone
19 long,] ~;
22 Kings] King's
40 refus'd] refus'de
52 *pase*] *Pass* G; *Pace* G2
55 *Princesse*] *Princesse'*

IV, iii

55 Budget,] ~;
77 *Swetnams*] *Swetnam's*

IV, iv

3 Kings] King's
4 SD∧] *points to her head decapitated.*
5 sight that] sight, That

IV, v

18 you? Oh] you? oh
41 Fields,] ~;
45 resum'd] reassum'd
48 onely] onelie
50 long,] ~;
59 Holland,] ~;
72 impossible,] ~;
78 Earth,] ~;
82 send] sends
84 beast,] ~;
101 afflictions.] ~:
103 Naples—] ~,
109 life:] ~;
119 Slaue,] ~;
125 Messenger,] ~;
138 accident?] ~;
139 SD∧] *giues a letter.*
140-141 To . . . Sex.] 'To . . . Sex.'
143-145 "Magnanimous . . . beautie."] 'Magnanimous . . . beautie.'
146-148 "Rather . . . Metamorphosis."] 'Rather . . . Metamorphosis.'
150-153 "In . . . you."] 'In . . . you.'
155-157 "To . . . *Misogynist.*"] 'To . . . *Misogynist.*'

155 contrition,] ~;
160 oportunitie.] opportuntie.
167 womans] woman's

V, i

18 should] shoulld
28 heat,] ~;
32 Deaths] Death's
34 Scholler,] schooler,
35 Teachers] Teacher's
52 Fathers] Father's
59 ask'd] ask't
79 hers,] her's,
117 carefully$_\wedge$] ~,
118 Kings] King's
127 ha.] ~!

V, ii

17 awhile,] ~.
31-32 too;/Nothing] too; Nothing
32 Spirit. Fall] Spirit./Fall
43 then?] G2; ~,   Sirrah!] ~? G; ~, G2
82 ha.] ~!
91 Sir?] ~.
112 SD$_\wedge$] *Strikes him still.*
122 you?] G2; your
142 ho.] ~!
154 to match] too mutch
160 oh.] ~!
172 oh.] ~!
176 oh.] ~!
181 Oh.] ~!
183 Oh.] ~!
185 oh.] ~!
187 oh.] ~!
197 once,$_\wedge$] ~ for
209 oh.] ~!
213 I,] ~$_\wedge$
228 full,] ~$_\wedge$
239 bite y'are] ~, y'ad
253 forsooth,] ~;
265 guiltie?] ~.
292 *The . . . women.*] "The . . . women."
296 write,] ~;
303 Champions,] ~:
322 Land,] ~;
335-336 Rascall./Forbeare] Rascall! Forbeare
340 oh.] ~!

V, iii

11 title] Q; ti [t] le
19 Subiects] Subiect's
21-22 prepar'd:/ Prepared to] prepar'd∧/∧To
22-23 you,/To] you, to
43 not in] G2; not good in
51 meaning,] ∼ ∧
68 meant by] G2; ∼ for
70 Follies.] ∼:
74 false] False
100 too,] ∼:
106 wonne,] ∼;
110-111 accepted./Imbrace] G2; accepted, imbrace
111 rise: neuer] G2; rise:/Neuer
111-112 late/To] G2; late to
116 mens] men's
120 Siluan's] siluan's
134 *Hymens*] *Hymen's*
144 doe? Good] G2; doe?/Good
167 aliue?] ∼.
190 *Leon.*] *Princess.*
191 life,] ∼;
192 lifes] life's
197 Fames] Fame's
198 her,] ∼!
209 Graces] Grace's

Epilogue

9 *life:*] ∼ ∧
11 *tyrannous, nor*] *tyrannous* ∧ *or*

Textual Notes

I, i

31 And . . . die,] Although there are seven feet in this line, I have made no attempt to reline because the preceding and following lines scan conventionally. There are many irregular lines in the play.

40 3. *Lord.*] This is probably a reference to the third lord, Sforza, for two reasons: (1) Sforza, though present as we learn later in 1. 84, has yet to speak, and is, in the context of the play, the lord of third importance; and (2) it would be foolish in such a scene of grief to have the three lords speak this line together.

83/84 SD] I have deleted the stage direction, *Enter Nicanor.*, for the obvious reason that Nicanor is already on stage, and the sense of the speech here is more or less agreeable with the change. There is the slightest possibility that Atticus was meant to call after Nicanor as he is leaving the stage, and then to turn to address the other two lords. In that case we would have been able to accept *Exit Nicanor.* as a plausible emendation. This latter suggestion has the advantage of getting Nicanor off stage now and avoiding the otherwise necessary quick exit and entrance suggested in 1. 95.

95 *Exit . . . Re-enter.*] See note on 1. 84 above. Obviously, Nicanor must exit at some time to learn of the soldier's arrival which he announces in 1. 98.

106-107 SD *A Flourish . . . . Scanfardoe.*] This change is justified for two reasons: (1) Scanfardo is not a lord and the Q reading, therefore, must be wrong. (Scanfardo, however, must be brought on stage for the conversation with Nicanor which closes the scene, 11. 183 ff.) and (2) Atticus' previous request that Sforza bring in the soldier demands that he, not Scanfardo, be designated here.

I, ii

16-20 A Spirit? . . . vprore.] I have retained the lineation of Q here although there is room for argument that this speech is prose, intentionally or not. Many of the speeches are irregular, and especially Swash's, some of which are obviously prose. It is, of course, common enough to give clowns and more "common" characters prose speeches.

87-88 you now./Ile] Grosart's emendation to "you;/Now" provides each line with ten syllables. However, such rigor is unnecessary, and I believe the lines as they stand in Q read as well as they do in Grosart's version, if not better.

121-135 And . . . bad.] After much consideration I have allowed these lines to stand as they do in Q: they are not strictly verse, and yet some of them seem to scan, e.g. 123, 129, 130, and 133. The speech is poetic prose, if nothing else.

138-142 From . . . another?] Here also I have left the lines as they stand in Q, although the speech may very well be meant as prose.

174-177 I doted . . . that,] The easy relining of this passage, which appears as prose in Q, seems to leave no doubt that it was meant to be verse.

I, iii

111-112 consent,/And] I have allowed these to stand as two lines because of the end rhyme, and, besides, joining them would result in a hexameter. I have elsewhere, avoided joining lines which would result in hexameters.

II, i

11-12 For . . . subsists?] Grosart relines these to, "whom/My." However, the scansion of his first suggested line and the shortness of the second cause more irregularities than would result from leaving the lines as they appear in Q.

58-63 *Lisandro* . . . . *Nicanor?*] Although these lines can be lined into a kind of verse, I have decided, after much vacillation, to leave them as they stand in Q. Loretta speaks sometimes in verse, sometimes in prose; here she apparently speaks in both in the same speech, for ll. 55-57 scan. I have lined ll. 66-68 so that her speech closes in verse, although I am aware that great objection is possible.

84 ith'] This spelling is retained as it appears in Q. Grosart suggests "i'th" which is acceptable and in some ways more plausible. However, I see no reason to assume a printer's error. No matter how it is written, there are two ellipses and only one mark.

161 I doe . . . Orator.] This line has six feet, but the two speeches seem meant to be one line of verse because of the easy rhythmic transition between "Honour" and "Be."

II, ii

Scene ii] I have chosen to begin a new scene here because of the obvious location shift to where Leonida is kept guarded.

25 As . . . thus:] These lines are irregular, but I have chosen to line them as verse. The arrangement of the latter half implies an effective, one-line introduction to the following prose. The contrast might have been, and might still be, useful to the actor speaking the lines.

100-112 Come . . . minute.] This speech is prose, but except for ll. 111 and 112, I have kept the lineation of Q.

124-163 But as . . . stealth.] Much of this is left as it stands in Q not because scansion dictates that it is poetry, but because the diction is poetic, and because there seems to have been some attempt by the playwright to give these lines meter. See, for instance, l. 132. The preceding lines, however, do not scan. Also, ll. 142-143 are clearly poetry. We can assume, reasonably, that some characters, especially those such as Loretta and Scanfardo, speak sometimes in poetry and sometimes in prose. See note II, i, 58-63.

II, iii

26 From . . . transgression.] Following l. 26 in Q is the stage direction, "*Enter* Nicanor." Later, following l. 30 is the direction retained here, "*Enter* Nicanor *and a guard.*" It is possible that the first direction, instead of being merely an error, represents the playwright's or director's intention that Nicanor enter so that he be seen by the audience but not by Lisandro and Leonida.

Such staging would be possible on the Elizabethan or Jacobean stage: Nicanor could enter from either of the rear doors while the action is taking place downstage, or he might appear in the inner stage while the lovers are talking.

III, i

31 *A Barre.*] Grosart notes that "[t]his is a warning to have ready the bar to which Lisandro and Leonida are to be brought on the next page. Such directions are common on the margin of old Plays, and are generally taken to show that the Play was printed from the Prompters' copy" (88). See the discussion in chapter two.

44-45 *Enter . . . Gard.*] These two stage directions are each two lines and side by side in Q.

120-121 The . . . end,] Although the lines stand divided here as they are in Q, they might stand as one line of iambic pentameter if the following ellisions were allowed: "the midd' and th'end."

III, ii

118 SD Loretta] I have made the change from *A Woman* because of the speech following the direction which designates that Loretta is reading the proclamation. Grosart suggests that the speech heading be changed to designate a herald reading the proclamation, "unless we suppose Loretta to be the herald" (xlvii). Loretta's presence in the herald's role would be consistent with the action of the play, especially in light of her part in the "arraignment" later of Swetnam.

141 baser] Grosart suggests that "basest" might go well here. At first he suggests that the "base" in 140 be "basest," but changes his mind in his notes (xlvii). I have chosen "baser" to contrast with "base" in l. 140. Also, this change supports the scansion of the line. (However, leaving Q's "base" in l. 140 does not particularly aid the scansion of that line.)

III, iii

3 SD Leonida] See chapter two for a discussion of the presence in Q of "Hortensia" here and a similar designation at III, iii, 140.

IV, i

13 pray'] Grosart omits the apostrophe in his text, but suggests that it "should have been retained, as it marks a contraction from *pray you*. The putting of apostrophes in place of personal pronouns is the subject of a chapter in W. S. Walker's valuable Criticism on Shakespeare" (xlviii).

54-56 Truth . . . Sir.] I believe this relining achieves greater regularity than does Q's, but it has the disadvantage of giving l. 54 six feet. Q's lineation allows three irregular lines; however, since they are short, the Q arrangement is perhaps more defensible.

IV, ii

22 house] Grosart suggests that "for house, the author perhaps wrote choise" (xlix).

IV, iv

Scene iiii and Scene v. I have designated two scenes here and thus implied that the two gentlemen are speaking at a location different from that place at which Lisandro and his two guards find Leonida's body, some eleven lines later. The problem here is more a play director's than an editor's, and one that can be solved easily in a number of ways by any given director; he could, for instance, simply omit the two gentlemen altogether, although this scene adds to the effectiveness of the drama. The difficulty arises from the question: are the two gentlemen speaking about Leonida's *body* or her *situation* when they comment on "the wofull'st sight that ere mine eyes beheld" (5), "a sight of griefe and horrour" (6), and "a piece of the extremest Iustice" (7)? The line of the second gentleman, "for instance see" (4), at least implies that he is pointing out some object for the first gentleman to look at. If this is Leonida's body (and the conventions of the Elizabethan and Jacobean stage, and these particular lines, certainly make one suspect that the author means to amuse the audience with the sight of the body), how can the body be headless when we know that Leonida appears whole and alive later? To further lead us to believe that the body is not in the gentlemen's presence, when Lisandro later grieves for the apparent death of his loved one, he says,

> See what a beauteous forme she yet retaynes,
> In despight of Fate, that men may see,
> Death could not seize but on her mortall parts: (28-30)

Are the gentlemen perhaps looking at the king's written decree?

Grosart, also confused, includes the following stage direction in his edition: *"points to her head decapitated."* However, he notes in his introduction, "Perhaps the (added) stage direction is wrong. Certainly the Princess's head was not really off, but someone else's head was shown as hers . . . . But then lower down . . . Lisandro is shown 'All that is left of faire *Leonida,*' i.e., . . . her corpse" (xlix). However, if her body is there at all, it must be there without a head, because they talk about the certainty of her beheading. I have chosen to add a stage direction in the next scene designating that a guard reveal Leonida's body (v, 11); thus, I imply that the body is not in the gentlemen's presence and that their attention is focused on some other prop, most likely the king's decree. This addition may rightfully be called arbitrary.

I believe we should make one further consideration: on ll. 44 and 45 Lisandro says, "Me thinkes, I feele fresh heat, as if her soule/ Had resum'd her former seate agen." In light of the fact that she is still alive, it is likely that the body really is radiating heat, and these lines reflect the common literary device of subtly forecasting what the audience is not to learn until later.

IV, v

11 *Reveals her body.*] See note for scenes iiii and v.

66 Princess] Grosart says that "Princes" could still stand for Princess, but that the word "as likely . . . ought to be written Princes'" (xlix).

116-119 But . . . Slaue?] These lines can be read in at least two ways. The "question mark" which I have chosen to retain may not be preferred, depending a great deal on one's interpretation of "But for." The expression could mean "except for," read, perhaps, with a sense of despair, or it could mean "however, for," which could be read with a feeling of determination. In this latter case, perhaps an exclamation point should replace the question mark at the end of l. 119. There is also the possibility that Q's comma at the close of l. 115 should be retained to indicate a closer relationship with the following lines which, in this case, would explain Atticus' lack of mercy. I doubt this latter possibility, for the king was indicating "justice" over "mercy" long before Misogenos debated.

V, i

Act V, Scene i] Grosart (xlix) also believes that Act V should begin here. Q designates Scene ii, 129 lines following this division.

98 dead! all dead!] The question mark, used often where modern practice calls for an exclamation mark, could be retained. One possible dramatic interpretation (one I frankly prefer) allows effective use of the oral interrogative inflection in contrast with the following declarative sentences. However, because retention of Q's punctuation might not bring the choice as readily to the reader's attention, I have emended. Also, I suspect the exclamation inflection was the author's intention.

111-116 This . . . Court.] Although Grosart allows these lines to stand as prose in Q, he notes later that "Nicanor's speech is six lines of blank verse" (xlix). I assume that he would have lined them as I have.

117 Iago.] Grosart overlooked the omission of this name heading when he prepared his text, but having later noticed that *Iag.* is the catchword on the recto page of H4, he indicated in a note (xlix) that the heading should be added.

V, ii

33-37 A sweet . . . you.] I have left these lines basically as they are in Q at the suggestion of Professor Arthur E. Barker who observes that they seem to represent a verse of a current drinking song.

43 Sirrah!] The exclamation mark here could be left a question mark if we are to take the "Sirrah" to be part of the address to Atlanta. Grosart, in his text, revises to "then, Sirrah?", but in his notes he revises again because, he says, Misogenos would not be so familiar with a woman, although addressing a woman in this way would not have been unusual. His second revision is to "then? Sirrah," (xlix).

165 and 177 *Young Woman.*] I have taken the liberty of changing the name heading from *A Boy.* for two reasons: (1) besides Misogenos and Swash, only women are present according to a previous stage direction, and *A Boy.* might well be referring to the actual boy who would be playing a woman's part; and (2) *Old Woman.* and *Scold.* seem carefully differentiated from *A Boy.*; therefore, the latter is probably not just a redundant reference to one of the men playing those women.

189-193 I . . . deuillishly.] These lines could, with justification, be run together as prose. But, again I believe we have prose mixed with poetry. See also ll. 203-207.

309 Vniuersitie] Although I seriously considered leaving the Q reading, "Niniuersitie," I finally decided that this was more likely a printer's error than a playwright's joke. Grosart guesses that "The corruption . . . was probably intentional, being put into the mouth of an ignorant character" (1).

V, iii

24 is't hee?] Grosart suggests that possibly this should be *metri gratia*, "is it hee?" (1).

60 *Sforz.*] There is a choice here of emending Q's *King.* to either *Iago.* or *Sforz.* or continuing it as Nicanor's speech. I have chosen Sforza because Iago is with Aurelia out of the king's sight. However, an interesting stage effect might be possible by giving the lines to Iago. A director might choose to do so. That the lines are meant to be Iago's to Aurelia is a possibility, one that would be consistent with the pattern hinted at on ll. 76-78 when Nicanor, the king, and Iago speak, in that order, further explaining the masque.

97 See how] To the left of these words in Q is the name heading, *Nic.*, but the speech obviously belongs to the king; it would make no sense in Nicanor's mouth.

175 old man?] Is this line addressed to the old silvan (i.e., Lorenzo), or to Iago? The scene seems to imply strongly the former. But the possibility of its being to Iago should not be overlooked. What most likely happens is that Aurelia addresses Lorenzo who is disguised as Atlanta who is disguised as a silvan.

190 *Leon.*] There seems no need to shift the speech heading policy at this point in the play. *Prince.* is the speech heading here probably because the playwright, the actors, or the printer anticipated the "princely" one word later. Also, this is the first time, in front of the characters in the play, that the prince and princess have been paired as such. They are in disguise the rest of the time. No matter the reason, the sense of the lines makes the speaker's identity certain.

Glossarial and Explanatory Notes

Act I, Scene i

4 a vertuous . . . Prince,] Grosart says that there is "little doubt that in the opening of our Play, the lamented Prince Henry (son of James I.) was in the recollection of the poet" (xlii). However, Henry died on November 6, 1612, and the play was written no earlier than 1616, and probably as late as 1618 or 1619.

30 begun] The use of "begun" and not "began" as the past tense form is really no surprise during this period. Grosart's comment on this phenomenon is interesting: "we should say 'began'; but curiously enough 'begun' still flourishes across the Atlantic. *e.g.,* in Mark Twain's *A Tramp Abroad* . . . we thus read—'When I first *begun* to understand jay language,' &c." (85-86). See also II, i, 81 and III, i, 52.

123 Lepanthean battel] Grosart notes that because of the date of the Battle of Lepanto, 1571, "there would have been historical inconsistency in introducing it into a Play written after 1617; but it is used adjectively, not nominally, and so is = the Lepanto-like battle" (86). However, there is no reason to believe that the battle referred to is not the Battle of Lepanto itself, especially in consideration of I, iii, 79-82:

> That he is dead, or in Captiuitie.
> For when *Don Iohn,* the Spanish Generall,
> Went with an Armie 'gainst the cruell Turkes,
> In that still memorable Battell of Lepanto, . . .

If one wished to date the setting of the play more specifically, he might consider I, i, 67-68:

> No, I shall neuer see *Lorenzo* more,
> This eighteene moneths I haue not heard of him; . . .

Thus, we could date the setting as sometime late in 1572 or early in 1573; however, such a concern is not very important to this play. The concern with Swetnam, after all, would give the play a contemporary setting; conflict in this matter is unavoidable and inconsequential.

152 It . . . want:] Grosart notes that these lines are "a skit on the times in which the Play was acted" (86). These are not the only lines which seem to comment on contemporary social conditions.

I, ii

2 By this,] i.e., by this time.

2 prest] i.e., published,

14 imbost] i.e., foaming at the mouth. Grosart notes that it is used "in the same sense as in *Taming of the Shrew,* Induction [l. 17]" (xlvi).

Glossarial and Explanatory Notes   155

43 one . . . me,] This could be a reference to either Ester Sowernam who wrote *Ester hath hang'd Haman* (1617) or Rachel Speght who wrote *A Mouzell for Melastomus* (1617). The former is the more biting and more effective of the two pamphlets, but, during the "arraignment" of Misogynos, one of his pseudonyms is said to be "Molastomus" (V, ii, 256).

57 *Bristow*,] See the discussion of Swetnam's biography in chapter one. The real Joseph Swetnam probably lived in Bristol at one time. Cf. V, ii, 315.

74 *Puncto*] i.e., punto, a thrust or foin.

93 *Callis Sands*.] Grosart notes that "the dramatist has forgotten that his scene is not laid in England" (xlvi).

120 Cullices] i.e., bouillon or meat broth, strained.

133 marry . . . these:] Cf. the following lines from Swetnam's pamphlet: "There are six kindes of women which thou shouldest take heede that thou match not thy selfe to any one of them, that is to say, good nor bad, faire nor foule, rich nor poore" (37).

153 if all . . . Paper;] Cf. in the *Araignment*: "therefore if all the world were paper, and all the sea inke, and all the trees and plants wer [sic] pens, and euery man in the world were a writer, yet were they not able with all their labour and cunning to set downe all the crafty deceits of women" (34-35).

165 Hackneyes,] At one place in the *Araignment* Swetnam refers to woman as "a common hackney for euery one that will ride" (32) and at another he says, "If thou marriest a still and a quiet women, that will seeme to thee that thou ridest but an ambling horse to hell but if with one that is froward and vnquiet, then thou wert as good ride a trotting horse to the deuil" (36).

178 I haue . . . all,] Here is an obvious reference to Swetnam's *Araignment*. If the number of editions and reprintings that the pamphlet went through is any test, the audience needed little help remembering what he had written.

I, iii

46 Pirean Mountaines,] This must be a reference to the Pyrenean Mountains. Grosart queries, "Pyranean" (87)?

82 Battell of Lepanto,] Grosart insists "an author's slip—'Lepanthean' as before . . . would have saved it here also" (87). See the comment on I, i, 123.

II, i

62 wee . . . too.] This statement relates to the controversy because it implies that men have set bad examples for women to follow. See Atlanta's argument that men are at fault because they lead women astray, that the wax is not at fault for the imprint on it (III, iii, 66-80). See also the "combat of generousity," when Lisandro says, "For what can Women aboue weaknesse act" (III, i, 63)? However, we seem to have more than just a reference to the feminist question. Probably this is either a topical reference or a general comment on the times, the corruption among the upper classes. Loretta, later, will use Leonida's going off alone with Lisandro as an excuse to invite Scanfardo to her chamber, "Hauing so good a president as I haue" (II, ii, 109). Grosart says l. 62 "seems a passing allusion" (xlii) to Lord Bacon's alleged bribe taking in court.

II, ii

24 Crist-Crosse row.] i.e., the alphabet.

43 fraughts] i.e., supplies, furnishes.

III, i

14 Father and a Friend,] Is Atticus making a general statement? *Father* refers to his relationship to Leonida, but can *Friend* refer to Lisandro if we are to believe what he says in I, i, 171-174 about being on poor terms with Lisandro's father?

145-158 My Lord . . . downe.] This fight between Iago and Nicanor probably should not occur in front of the king. One would think that such an argument would take place behind the king's back, for reasons of both court protocol and play production. Surely, Atticus would take Iago's charge under consideration. Instead, he ignores an argument between two of his closest advisers, an argument which promises to end in civil war. I have not, as I was tempted to, emended with a stage direction to have the important part of the argument take place to one side, away from the king, who might be pantomiming discussion with the judges. Perhaps, in light of Atticus' disapproval later of Iago, he should ignore them here with a despairing shrug or sigh. However, most likely the argument moved down stage to the front of the platform while action stood still or went on silently behind.

155 timeless] i.e., untimely or ill-timed.

III, ii

25-29 For . . . auoyded.] Cf. the *Araignment's* "they are vngratefull, periured, full of fraud, flouting and deceit, vnconstant, waspish, toyish, light, sullen, proude, discurteous and cruell, and yet they were by God created, and by nature formed, and therefore by pollicy and wisedome to be auoyded" (20).

52 Be-spawld] i.e., spat upon. The *NED* definies it, "To bespatter with saliva."

III, iii

7 vnequall] i.e., unjust, unfair. Cf. "equall," III, iii, 46.

7 impartiall] The *NED* says that the word is "misused for partial," and it cites the quotation from *Swetnam the Woman-hater* and one other from *Romeo and Juliet*. The prefix might have been meant as an intensifier. Cf. III, iii, 262.

46 equall] See III, iii, 7.

89-90 And . . . Sunne.] It was, of course, Dedalus' son, not daughter, who flew too close to the sun. Is Swetnam's lack of learning, as well as the irony of the implication, meant to be shown here?

159 Stale] i.e., a common prostitute, one who is used to decoy men in order that they can be robbed by accomplices.

167 Vp-sittings,] Grosart notes "that which celebrates the first uprising of the woman from bed," citing Halliwell, "In the North, the first party after an accouchement" (88).

200 veney] i.e., veny, a fencing thrust.

227-228 The Kalender . . . vp] This is a very common anti-feminist accusation which Swetnam's *Araignment* implies but never really makes use of.

262 impartiall] See the note on III, iii, 7.

276 A King . . . Starre,] This is similar to Caesar's speech to the senate just before he is killed: "But I am constant as the Northern Star" (III, i, 60).

IV, ii

44 *Quid . . . soll.*] It is difficult to suggest what this might be. Grosart notes, "The first two words might be a (Latin) technical phrase 'Quid inde,' &c.=What's that to me? What of that? and then the musical notes 'do re me fa so la, &c., as a kind of lilt or trill expressive of joy" (li).

IV, iii

40 forc't] Grosart queries Q's forecast: "misprint for 'forced'? . . . oddly spelled 'forcest' or forc't?" (89).

65 A Masculine Feminine?] An appropriate term in a play treating the feminist issue. "Masculine feminines" and "feminine masculines" were themselves the subjects of pamphlets at this time.

IV, v

61 warres . . . them.] There may have been some attempt by the playwright to set the date of the action at the earlier time of the Battle of Lepanto. This reference seems to be to wars that the audience knows have already taken place. See note on I, i, 123.

V, ii

45 SD *Offers some food.*] This stage direction is deliberately vague. Atlanta may give food or wine to Swash to consume as he stands aside, or she may offer something to Misogenos to keep him occupied and away from her. The latter seems more probable, funnier at any rate.

74 such a foole?] The meaning of this exchange is somewhat mysterious. Why does Misogenos say, "Doe you thinke me such a foole?" Is it necessary for Atlanta to get off stage so that the exchange between Swash and Misogenos in the next scene can reveal that Misogenos is a bigger rascal than he heretofore has shown himself, that his previous profession of love-sickness was false, and that his love waned easily on the threshold of fulfillment? The best answer may be that she whispers that he be sure to get rid of Swash. Thus, she is motivated to leave while he performs this task discreetly, and we are allowed to witness Misogenos denying the sincerity of his love. This guess is further supported by Atlanta's question, "Are you in priuate, Sir" (91)? when she reenters.

122 a Fencer?] These lines, which seem suspiciously like lines to be delivered by several persons, may be here to show surprise on even Lorenzo's part that Misogenos is as bad a fencer as he is.

128 stale] This word is probably used in the same sense as III, iii, 159, meaning a prostitute of the lowest class.

133 sowre sauce] Cf. Swetnam's pamphlet, "For although they seem to be so dainty as sweet meat, yet in tryall not so wholesome as sowre sauce: they haue wit, but it is all in craft; if they loue, it is vehement, but if they hate it is deadly" (20).

167 Post and Paire] This is a card game also called Post. The *NED* quotes Nares: "A game on the cards, played with three cards each, wherein much depended on the goodness of your own hand."

184 revy'd] i.e., revie or raise.

256 *Alias Molastomus*] This is the name given Swetnam in Rachel Speght's *Mouzell for Melastomus* (1617). See note on I, ii, 43.

296 You . . . write,] Recall that Swetnam published his book under the pseudoym of "Th. Tel-troth."

300 He is no Fencer,] There is no evidence that the real Joseph Swetnam was not a legitimately competent fencer.

321 Till . . . spight,] Here is another reference to Ester Sowernam and Rachel Speght who wrote answers to Swetnam's pamphlet. Professor Bentley, v, 1417, suggests the possibility that "spight" might be a play on "Speght."

342 let . . . burn'd] These lines seem to be both an invitation to a printer and the playwright's legitimate boast, implying that the play is much superior to the pamphlet, as indeed it is. The irony here, however, is that the play was published in 1620 and not again until 1880 when Grosart edited it. The pamphlet was published again and again throughout the seventeenth century and into the eighteenth. See chapter one.

V, iii

90 But . . . them.] Atticus probably means that the allegorical characters of the masque have real shape within his mind, and he will suffer sleepless nights because he is guilty of the faults they represent.

164-165 Which thus . . . all.] Just what the king is doing here is not clear. Probably he is embracing them. However, l. 165 remains obscure: it may mean simply that after the step to which he refers, the masque must be called to an end, or, improbably, that the king is ready to end his life.

Epilogue

15 *Mercie . . . sympathize:*] It is perhaps significant that mercy and beauty are usually thought of as feminine traits; Mercy, of course, in the morality tradition, is a daughter of God.

21 *my sword . . . defence.*] Recall that the Swetnam of the play was not a swordsman, but only pretended to be.

Bibliography

The following is a selected bibliography, mostly of works which mention or touch upon the subject of the controversy or the play itself. Many other works have been consulted, most standard for editions of renaissance literature.

Bentley, Gerald Eades. *The Jacobean and Caroline Stage.* 5 vols. Oxford, 1941-1956.

Bradford, Gamaliel. *Elizabethan Women.* ed. Harold Ogden White. Cambridge, Mass., 1936.

Camden, Charles Carroll. *The Elizabethan Woman.* Houston, 1952.

Chambers, E. K. *The Elizabethan Stage.* 4 vols. London, 1923.

Creizenach, Wilhelm. *English Drama in the Age of Shakespeare,* tr. from *Geschichte des neueren dramas.* London, 1916.

Dictionary of National Biography. 63 vols. and supplements. London, 1885-.

Fleay, Frederick G. *A Chronicle History of the London Stage, 1559-1642.* London, 1890.

Greg, W. W. *Bibliography of the English Printed Drama.* 4 vols. Oxford, 1939-59.

Greg, W. W. *Dramatic Documents From the Elizabethan Playhouses.* 2 vols. Oxford, 1931.

Greg, W. W. *A List of English Plays Written Before 1643 and Printed before 1700.* London, 1899.

Greg, W. W. and E. Boswell, eds. *Records of the Court of the Stationers' Company, 1576 to 1662 from Register B.* London, 1930.

Grosart, Alexander B., ed. "Swetnam the Woman-hater," with notes, illustrations and facsimiles, *Occasional Issues,* XIV. Manchester, England, 1880.

Harbage, Alfred. *Annals of English Drama.* Revised ed. by S. Schoenbaum. London, 1964.

Harbage, Alfred. *Cavalier Drama.* New York, 1936.

Langbaine, Gerard. *An Account of the English Dramatick Poets.* Oxford, 1961. Revised by C. Gildon, et al., *The Lives and Characters of the English Dramatick Poets.* Reissued, 1699.

Lawrence, William J. *Pre-Restoration Stage Studies.* Cambridge, 1927.

Matulka, Barbara. *The Novels of Juan de Flores and their European Diffusion.* New York, 1931.

Munda, Constantia. *The worming of a mad Dogge, or a Soppe for Cerberus.* London, 1617.

Murray, John Tucker. *English Dramatic Companies 1558-1642.* 2 vols. New York, 1910.

Reynolds, George Fulmer. *The Staging of Elizabethan Plays at the Red Bull Theater, 1605-1625.* London, 1940.

Schelling, Felix E. *Elizabethan Drama 1558-1642.* 2 vols. Boston and New York, 1908.

Sowernam, Ester. *Ester hath hang'd Haman.* London, 1617.

Speght, Rachel. *A Mouzell for Melastomus.* London, 1617.

Swetnam, Joseph. *The Araignment of Lewde, idle, froward, and vnconstant women.* London, 1615.

Swetnam, Joseph. *The Schoole of the noble science of defence.* London, 1617.

Tuvil, Daniel. *Asylum Veneris.* London, 1616.

Wright, Louis B. *Middle-Class Culture in Elizabethan England.* Chapel Hill, 1935.

Index

In the following index the lower case letters, n, gn, *and* tn *represent* Footnotes, Glossarial and Explanatory Notes, *and* Textual Notes, *respectively.*

Account of the English Dramatick Poets, An, 31n, 159b
Aggas, Edward, 31n
Aletiphilo, Lelio, 25, 31n
Annals of English Drama, 159b
Araignment Of Lewde, idle, froward, and vnconstant women, The, 1, 2, 3, 4, 6, 10, 20n, 31n, 155gn, 156gn, 160b
Asylum Veneris, 4, 5, 20n, 21n, 160b
Aurelio and Isabel, 21n, 22, 25, 30, 31n

Barker, Professor Arthur E., 152tn
Bentley, Gerald B., 19, 21n, 27-28, 31n, 32n, 46n, 158gn, 159b
Bibliography of the English Printed Drama, 32n, 52n, 159b
Biographical Chronicle of the English Drama 1599-1642, A, 32n
Bradford, Gamaliel, 159b

Caesar, Julius, 157gn
Camden, Charles Carroll, 21n, 159b
Captives, The, 30
Cavalier Drama, 159b
Chambers, E.K., 27, 32n, 159b
Chronicle History of the London Stage, A, 159b
Collier, J.P., 40, 46n
Creizenach, Wilhelm, 159b
Criticism on Shakespeare, 150tn

Dedalus, 156gn
De Flores, Juan, 11, 12, 21n, 22, 26, 31n, 33
Dekker, Thomas, 28
Dictionary of National Biography, 159b
Dramatic Documents From the Elizabethan Playhouses, 159b
Dramatic Works, 32n
Drewe, Thomas, 28
Duchess of Malfi, The, 46n

Editorial Problem in Shakespeare, The, 32n
Elizabethan Drama 1558-1642, 32n, 160b
Elizabethan Stage, The, 32n, 159b
Elizabethan Woman, The, 21n, 159b
Elizabethan Women, 159b
English Drama in the Age of Shakespeare, 159b
English Dramatic Companies, 32n, 159b
Ester hath hang'd Haman, 4, 7, 9, 11, 20-21n, 155gn, 160b

Farmer, J.S., 48, 52n
Female Rebellion, 29
Fleay, F.G., 26, 32n, 159b
Fletcher, John, 29

Geschichte des neueren dramas, 159b
Gildon, C. et al, 31n
Golden Age, 28
Greg, W.W., 30, 32n, 50, 52n, 159b
Grisel Y Mirabella, 21n, 22, 26, 31n
Grosart, Alexander B., 1, 4, 20n, 21n, 22, 26, 28, 30, 31n, 32n, 43, 46n, 48, 49, 50-51, 141, 148tn, 149tn, 150tn, 151tn, 152-153tn, 154gn, 155gn, 156gn, 157gn, 158gn, 159b
Grosart's Emendations, Table of, 49, 141-147, 148tn

Harbage, Alfred, 32n, 159b
Heywood, Thomas, 28-29, 30, 32n
Historia de Aurelio e Isabella, 21n, 22, 31n
Historia de Aurelia, Isabella Hija del Reyde Escotia, & C., 31n
History of English Dramatic Poetry, The, 46n

Index of Printers, Publishers and Booksellers, 32n

Jacobean and Caroline Stage, The, 21n, 159b
Julius Caesar, 15

Langbaine, Gerard, 22, 31n, 159b
Latio, Juan, 31n
Lawrence, William J., 159b
Lepanto, Battle of, 154gn
List of English Plays Written before 1643 and Printed Before 1700, A, 159b
Lives and Characters of the English Dramatick Poets, The, 31, 159b

Matulka, Barbara, 1, 12, 20n, 21n, 22, 25-26, 27, 31n, 32n, 159b
Meighen, Richard, 48, 51
Middle-Class Culture in Elizabethan England, 20n, 160b
Mommart, Jean, 31n
Morrison, Paul G., 32n
Mouzell for Melastomus, A, 4, 6, 7, 20n, 26, 155gn, 158gn, 160b
Munda, Constantia, 4, 9-10, 11, 26, 159b
Murray, John Tucker, 27, 32n, 159b

Nabbes, Thomas, 27
Novels of Juan de Flores and Their European Diffusion, The, 20n, 159b

Occasional Issues, 20n, 159b

Pre-Restoration Stage Studies, 159b
Prince Henry (Son of James I), 154gn

Queen Anne, 18, 27
Queen Anne's players, 18, 26
Queen's Men, 28
Queen's Servants, 31n

Records of the Court of Stationers' Company, 1576 to 1662 from Register B, 159b
Red-Bull audience, 18-19, 21n, 34
Red Bull Theater, 18, 26, 28, 31, 33, 34, 51
Reynolds, George Fulmer, 21n, 27, 32n, 46n, 160b
Reyne, Jean, 31n
Romeo and Juliet, 156gn
Ruskin, 51

Salisbury Court Theatre, 27-28
Schelling, Felix, E., 26, 32n, 160b
Schoole of The Noble and Worthy Science of Defence, The, 1, 20n, 160b
Sea Voyage, The, 29
Sharp, Joane, 9
Sowernam, Ester, 4, 7-9, 10, 11, 155gn, 158gn, 160b
Speght, Rachel, 4, 6, 10, 27, 155gn, 158gn, 160b
Staging of Elizabethan Plays at the Red Bull Theater 1605-1625, The, 21n, 32n, 160b
Stansby, William, 32n, 50, 52n
Steelsio, Juan, 31n
Swetnam, Joseph, 1-2, 3, 4-5, 6, 7, 8, 9, 10, 11, 25, 26, 30, 33, 155gn, 157gn, 158gn, 160b

Taming of the Shrew, 154gn
Tel-troth, Thomas, 4, 158gn
Tottenham Court, 27
Tramp Abroad, A, 154gn
Tuvil, Daniel, 4, 5, 6, 8, 10, 11, 21n, 160b
Twain, Mark, 154gn

Walker, W.S., 150tn
Webster, John, 46n
White Devil, The, 46n
Worming of a mad Dogge, 4, 9-10, 11, 21n, 26, 159b
Wright, Louis B., 2-3, 20n, 21n, 29, 30, 32n, 160b

This book was printed in Garamond and Cloister Bold typefaces on Warren's Old Style 60 lb. paper by C. E. Pauley and Company, Indianapolis, Indiana, and casebound in Interlaken bookcloth by the H & H Bookbinding Company of Indianapolis. The dust jackets of Sorg's Parchtex were designed by Moroni J. St. John and printed by offset lithography by the Haywood Publishing Company of Lafayette, Indiana. Editorial and production supervision were by Eleanor Crandall and Diane Dubiel.